The *Pocket* VEGETABLE EXPERT

Dr. D. G. Hessayon

First edition: 120,000 copies
Published 2002
by Expert Books
a division of Transworld Publishers

Copyright © Dr.D.G.Hessayon 2002

The right of Dr.D.G.Hessayon to be identified
as author of this work has been asserted in accordance
with sections 77 and 78 of the Copyright Designs and
Patents Act 1988.

A catalogue record for this book is available from the British Library

TRANSWORLD PUBLISHERS
61-63 Uxbridge Road, London W5 5SA
a division of the Random House Group Ltd

  Distributed in the United States
by Sterling Publishing Co. Inc.,
387 Park Avenue South,
New York,
NY 10016-8810

EXPERT BOOKS

CONTENTS

Reproduction by Spot On Digital Imaging Ltd, Perivale, Middx. UB6 7JB
Printed and bound by GGP Media GmbH

ISBN 0 903505 57 6   © D.G. HESSAYON 2002

CHAPTER 1

INTRODUCTION

Rich and poor, north and south, mansion and cottage — millions of people grow vegetables and interest in picking one's own produce shows no sign of declining. The Vegetable Expert is the country's best selling gardening book and this Pocket version provides finger tip information when you are in the garden or on the allotment.

There are a number of reasons why people choose to grow vegetables. If your plot, home freezer and garden shed storage space are large enough you can aim to be almost self-sufficient, but this is not often the gardener's goal. An important motive is that you can harvest at the peak of tenderness and flavour instead of having to wait for maximum yields like the professional grower. In addition you can cook and serve these vegetables within an hour or two of picking — with sweet corn, beans and asparagus this means a new flavour experience. Another reason for growing your own is that you can produce vegetables which do not appear in the shops and you can grow varieties of ordinary vegetables which are not raised commercially. You can save money by growing your own but this is not the main motive for most people — it is just a bonus from a hobby which provides a special thrill from growing and then eating your own.

Most of the principles of vegetable growing have been with us for hundreds of years — some of the basics are as old as civilisation itself. But the subject doesn't stand still — in recent years the idea of growing vegetables in beds rather than on a traditional plot has taken root, and baby vegetable varieties are now listed in the popular catalogues. New varieties of standard vegetables appear every year but don't be too experimentally-minded — make sure you only grow those vegetables which the family like to eat. Finally, a word or two for beginners. Before you decide on growing a vegetable, make sure it is suitable for your site. If it is, then read the relevant section in the A - Z guide. The table on the first page will tell you the sort of yield you can expect — it is often possible to avoid a glut by sowing short rows at intervals. Be guided by the calendar — success depends on doing the right thing at the right time.

CHAPTER 2

VEGETABLES A - Z

Nearly all of the vegetables which can be grown in the garden are described in this chapter. Some are universal favourites — lettuce, carrots, beetroot, etc and others are much less popular. You will not find celeriac, kohl rabi nor aubergine on the average plot. No doubt the major part of your own seed order will be drawn from the group of favourites, and that is the way it should be. Do try some of the newer varieties, however, as improvements continue to appear.

WHAT THE CALENDAR SYMBOLS MEAN

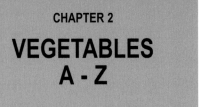

	Most popular time for sowing outdoors		Most popular time for transplanting garden-grown seedlings
	Less usual time for sowing outdoors. The earlier panel generally refers to S. England		Less usual time for transplanting garden-grown seedlings. The earlier panel generally refers to S. England
	Recommended time for sowing outdoors under cloches or in a cold frame		Recommended time for transplanting seedlings raised under glass
	Recommended time for sowing indoors under glass		Recommended time for transplanting seedlings raised under glass. Cover with cloches

Month	JAN	FEB	MAR	APR	MAY	JUN	JUL	AUG	SEP	OCT	NOV	DEC
Sowing Time												
Planting Time												
Lifting Time												

	Most popular time for harvesting
	Less usual time for harvesting

ARTICHOKE, GLOBE

A thistle-like plant which is at home in the herbaceous border. It grows over 1 m high with arching silvery leaves. The ball-like heads are removed for cooking just before the fleshy scales open. A fussy plant requiring good soil, regular watering, feeding and frost protection.

Productive life	4 years
Expected yield per mature plant	10 - 12 heads
Approximate time between planting and cutting	1½ years
Ease of cultivation	Not easy

CALENDAR

Month	JAN	FEB	MAR	APR	MAY	JUN	JUL	AUG	SEP	OCT	NOV	DEC
Sowing Time			▓	▓								
Planting Time				▓								
Cutting Time							▓	▓	▓	▓		

SOWING & PLANTING THE CROP

Seed is sown thinly 3 cm deep in drills 30 cm apart. Thin to 20 cm. Plant out in the following spring.

It is easier to start with offsets (rooted suckers) — about 20 - 25 cm in length with roots attached.

The site should be light or loamy soil in a sunny, sheltered location. Good drainage is essential. Dig in autumn and incorporate a liberal amount of compost or well-rotted manure. Rake in a general-purpose fertilizer shortly before planting.

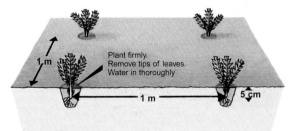

1 m

Plant firmly.
Remove tips of leaves.
Water in thoroughly

1 m

5 cm

LOOKING AFTER THE CROP

Keep the plants well watered until established. Apply a mulch around the stems in May. During the summer months hoe regularly and apply a liquid fertilizer at fortnightly intervals. Water thoroughly when the weather is dry.

In late autumn cut down the stems and cover the crowns with bracken, leaves or straw. Remove this protective covering in April.

HARVESTING THE CROP

A few small heads will begin to form in the first year. Do not let them develop — cut off immediately and discard.

Regular cropping begins in the season after planting. Remove the terminal bud first. It should be large and swollen but still green and unopened. Leave 5 - 8 cm of the stem attached.

Feed the plants after this first cropping. Later in the season remove and cook the secondary heads.

VARIETIES

You will find Green Globe in all the popular seed catalogues, but for the other varieties you will have to look through some of the specialist catalogues.

GREEN GLOBE The popular choice — produces large heads with a good flavour.

PURPLE GLOBE Hardier than its green relative and more eye-catching, but lower in flavour.

VERT DE LAON Noted for its reliability — received an Award of Merit from the Royal Horticultural Society.

VIOLETTA DI CHIOGGIA The one to grow from seed — the heads are an attractive purple.

Green Globe

Violetta di Chioggia

ASPARAGUS

Succulent young shoots appear in spring and are cut for the kitchen. Attractive ferny foliage is produced when they are left to develop but this should never be cut for flower arranging. Asparagus is not an easy crop — it needs thorough soil preparation, space and regular hand weeding. Well worth growing, however, if you have free-draining soil, adequate land which can be tied up for a decade or more and also patience — you will have to wait two years for your first hearty meal. Use 1-year-old crowns — you can buy 2- or 3-year-old crowns but they are temperamental. The traditional annual heavy dressing with manure is not necessary. Asparagus can also be raised from seed but it will be 3 years before regular cropping can begin and it really isn't worth losing a year.

Productive life	8 - 20 years
Expected yield per mature plant	20 - 25 spears
Time between planting 1-year crowns and cutting	2 years
Ease of cultivation	Not easy

CALENDAR

Plant crowns in early April if the soil is in good condition — delay for a couple of weeks if the soil is cold and wet. Trenches should be dug about 1 m apart.

Harvesting the mature crop takes place over a 6 - 8 week period. In order to ensure the longest possible harvesting season it is a good idea to plant a mixed bed containing an early variety such as Connovers Colossal with a later variety such as Martha Washington if you can find a supplier.

Month	JAN	FEB	MAR	APR	MAY	JUN	JUL	AUG	SEP	OCT	NOV	DEC
Sowing Time			▒	█								
Planting Time				█								
Cutting Time					█	▒						

7

SOWING & PLANTING THE CROP

Seed is sown thinly 3 cm deep in drills 30 cm apart. Thin to 15 cm when seedlings are 8 cm tall. Plant out the largest plants in the following spring.

You can save time by obtaining 1-year-old crowns ready for planting. The site should be free-draining, sunny and sheltered from strong winds. Dig thoroughly in autumn and incorporate a liberal dressing of well-rotted manure or compost. Liming will be necessary if the soil is very acid.

Remove the roots of all perennial weeds during soil preparation. Leave the soil rough after digging — fork over in March and rake in a general-purpose fertilizer.

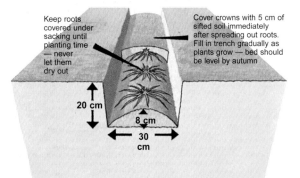

Keep roots covered under sacking until planting time — never let them dry out

Cover crowns with 5 cm of sifted soil immediately after spreading out roots. Fill in trench gradually as plants grow — bed should be level by autumn

20 cm

8 cm

30 cm

LOOKING AFTER THE CROP

Keep the beds clean by hand weeding. Provide support for the stems if necessary and water during dry weather. Remove any berries before they fall on the ground.

In autumn cut down the ferny stems when they turn yellow. Leave stumps 2 - 5 cm above the surface.

In spring make a ridge of soil over each row with a draw hoe before the spears appear. Apply a surface dressing of a general-purpose fertilizer.

HARVESTING THE CROP

Do not cut any of the spears which appear shortly after planting. In the year after planting little or no cutting should take place.

Cutting can begin in earnest in the second year after planting. As soon as the spears reach 10 - 15 cm they should be severed about 8 cm below the soil surface. Use a long serrated kitchen knife or a special asparagus knife. Cut every day if necessary — never let the spears grow too tall before cutting.

Stop cutting in early or mid June. All spears must now be allowed to develop into fern in order to build up reserves for next year's crop.

VARIETIES

The old varieties such as Connovers Colossal give rise to both male and female plants. The female ones are less productive and they also produce berries which are followed by unwanted seedlings.

The trend these days is to grow one of the all-male hybrids — you will find crowns offered by garden centres and in the seed catalogues. One or two are also available as seed.

CITO A French variety noted for its unusually long spears which appear early in the season. An all-male hybrid that yields heavily.

CONNOVERS COLOSSAL The old variety which is still widely available as seed and crowns. Thick-stalked and early, but crops less heavily than the F_1 all-male hybrids.

FRANKLIM An all-male hybrid with thick spears available as crowns and seed. You can cut a few spears in the year following planting.

GEYNLIM One of the modern all-male hybrids. Its main claim to fame is that it is available for cutting earlier than most others — grow in a mixed bed.

JERSEY KNIGHT Something different — the supplier claims that you can harvest some spears of this all-male hybrid in the season after sowing.

LUCULLUS The first of the all-male hybrids with the usual benefits — long and straight spears and heavy crops. It has slipped out of the popular catalogues.

MARTHA WASHINGTON The best known of the American varieties. A heavy cropper with long spears until early June. Resistant to rust.

PURPLE JUMBO Something different — an asparagus with purple spears. The novelty is lost when boiled — the spears change to ordinary green.

THEILIM This all-male hybrid is a recent introduction and crowns are offered in numerous catalogues. Suppliers claim high yields.

Connovers Colossal

Franklim

AUBERGINE

Aubergine is a shrubby plant which bears attractive flowers followed by oval or round fruit. It can be grown in a greenhouse as easily as a tomato, but outdoors it is much more of a gamble. It needs a sunny sheltered spot in a mild area of the country, and a long hot summer to ripen the fruit.

Expected germination time	14 - 21 days
Expected yield per plant	2 - 2.5 kg
Approximate time between sowing and picking	20 weeks
Ease of cultivation	Difficult outdoors

CALENDAR

Month	JAN	FEB	MAR	APR	MAY	JUN	JUL	AUG	SEP	OCT	NOV	DEC
Sowing & Planting Time (outdoor crop)			🪴🪴		🌱							
Sowing & Planting Time (greenhouse crop)		🪴		🌱🌱🌱🌱								
Picking Time												

SOWING & PLANTING THE CROP

Raise seedlings under glass at 15° - 20°C. Sow 2 seeds in a compost-filled peat pot — remove weaker seedling.

For outdoor cultivation well-drained fertile soil in a sunny, sheltered location is necessary. Add a general-purpose fertilizer before planting.

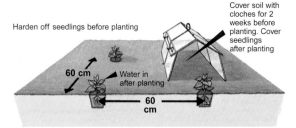

Cover soil with cloches for 2 weeks before planting. Cover seedlings after planting

Harden off seedlings before planting

60 cm

Water in after planting

60 cm

In the greenhouse grow in pots filled with compost — pot on to final 5 litre size. Alternatively plant in growing bags — 3 per bag. Plant in April (heated house) or early May (unheated).

LOOKING AFTER THE CROP

Remove the growing point when the plant is 30 cm high — stake stems. Mist plants regularly to keep down red spider mite and to encourage fruit set. Pinch out the first flower. For large fruits remove lateral shoots and any remaining flowers once 5 fruits have formed.

Water regularly but do not keep the compost sodden. Add a potassium-rich soluble fertilizer with each watering once the fruits have begun to swell.

HARVESTING THE CROP

Cut each fruit once it has reached a satisfactory size (usually about 15 cm long) but before the surface gloss has disappeared. Dull fruit are usually over-ripe and bitter.

VARIETIES

BAMBINO A novelty for the patio — 30 cm high plants with clusters of 3 cm long purple fruits.

BLACK ENORMA A rival to Slice Rite — the extra-large fruits appear early in the season.

BONICA An F_1 hybrid with a good reputation for reliability. Compact and bushy with oval purple fruits.

LONG PURPLE An old favourite which is one of the easiest to grow. Suitable for outdoor and greenhouse cultivation.

MONEYMAKER A modern favourite — this F_1 hybrid produces an early crop of good-sized fruits.

OVA Egg-sized white fruits — grow in a greenhouse or in a pot on the patio.

SLICE RITE The one to grow if you like giant vegetables — fruits can weigh 500 gm or more.

Long Purple

Slice Rite

BEAN, BROAD

This crop produces the first beans of the season and is one of the easiest vegetables to grow. Picking can begin as early as May if you pamper the crop, but even the maincrop sown in the ordinary way in April will be ready in July. Three or four square-sectional stems arise from each seed — standard varieties grow about 1.2 m high and the dwarfs reach 30 - 45 cm. The white-and-black flowers are followed by leathery pods with beans which are white or green.

Expected germination time	7 - 14 days
Approximate number per 100 gm	55
Amount required for a 3 m double row	55 gm
Expected yield from a 3 m double row	9 kg
Life expectancy of stored seed	2 years
Approximate time between autumn sowing and picking	26 weeks
Approximate time between spring sowing and picking	14 weeks
Ease of cultivation	Easy

CALENDAR

November sowing of Aquadulce Claudia or The Sutton will provide an early crop of beans in June, but there can be serious losses in a severe winter. Only attempt autumn sowing if your plot is sheltered, free-draining and in a mild area — for all other locations it is a better plan to sow under cloches in February.

Maincrop sowings begin in March and are then made at monthly intervals to the end of May to provide beans throughout the summer.

Month	JAN	FEB	MAR	APR	MAY	JUN	JUL	AUG	SEP	OCT	NOV	DEC
Sowing Time												
Picking Time												

12

SOWING THE CROP

Nearly any soil will produce an adequate crop, provided it is neither very acid nor waterlogged. Lime, if necessary, in winter. Choose a reasonably sunny spot which did not grow beans last year. Dig in autumn if the crop is to be sown in spring — add compost or well-rotted manure if the ground was not enriched for the previous crop. Apply a general-purpose fertilizer about 1 week before sowing. Discard all seeds which bear small, round holes.

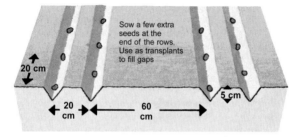

Sow a few extra seeds at the end of the rows. Use as transplants to fill gaps

20 cm

20 cm

60 cm

5 cm

LOOKING AFTER THE CROP

Regular hoeing will probably be necessary to keep down weeds during the early stage of the crop's life, but watering is unlikely to be necessary before the flowers appear.

Some form of support will probably be required for tall-growing varieties. Place a stout stake at each corner of the double row and then tie string between the posts at 30 cm intervals.

Pinch out the top 10 cm of stem as soon as the first beans start to form. This will ensure an earlier harvest and also provide some degree of control against blackfly. This serious pest must be kept down, so spray with an insecticide if attacks persist. If the weather turns dry when the pods are swelling it will be necessary to water copiously.

HARVESTING THE CROP

Remember that you are not trying to win a prize when you are growing broad beans for the kitchen. Leaving the pods to reach their maximum size will provide a glut of large and tough beans.

Begin picking when the first pods are 5 - 8 cm long — cook them whole.

The time to pick pods for shelling is when the beans have begun to show through the pod but before the scar on each shelled bean has become discoloured — it should still be white or green.

Remove each pod from the plant by applying a sharp downward twist. Dig the plants into the soil after cropping has finished to provide valuable green manure.

VARIETIES

LONGPOD varieties

Long narrow pods — 40 cm or more. 8 - 10 kidney-shaped beans. Best for hardiness, early cropping and high yields.

AQUADULCE CLAUDIA White. The popular choice for autumn sowing. Tall, prolific and very hardy. Good for freezing.

BUNYARD'S EXHIBITION White. Not the biggest, tastiest or heaviest cropper, but still one of the most reliable varieties.

HYLON White. One of the modern varieties which has staked a claim to be the longest-podded broad bean.

IMPERIAL GREEN LONGPOD Green. An old favourite noted for its extra-long pods and high yields.

MASTERPIECE GREEN LONGPOD Green. A popular early cropper with a fine flavour. Good for freezing.

RED EPICURE Reddish-brown. The beans turn yellow when boiled — steam to retain the red colour. Distinctive flavour.

STEREO White. Something different. Small pods with half-sized beans can be cooked and served like mangetout.

WITKIEM VROMA White. The Witkiem varieties are sown in early spring for a July crop. Broad well-filled pods.

WINDSOR varieties

Shorter and broader than Longpods. 4 - 7 round beans. Best for flavour, but not suitable for autumn sowing.

GREEN WINDSOR Green. A heavy cropper with deep green beans. Not suitable for early planting.

WHITE WINDSOR White. The basic white-seeded Windsor — newer varieties include Jubilee Mysor. Susceptible to frost.

DWARF varieties

Low-growing bushy plants. 3 - 5 kidney-shaped beans. Best for cloche-growing, exposed sites and mini-gardens.

THE SUTTON White. The most popular dwarf, producing an abundant crop of short pods with plump beans.

Hylon

The Sutton

BEAN, FRENCH

A half-hardy annual which likes warm conditions and hates heavy clay. The blooms are white, pink or red and it is decorative enough to be grown in the flower garden. Standard varieties are bushy plants with 10 - 15 cm long green pods, but there are variations. You can buy purple- or yellow-podded types as well as climbing varieties which can grow as tall as runner beans. In recent years there have been many introductions and seeds are now planted more closely than used to be advised in the textbooks.

Expected germination time	7 - 14 days
Approximate number per 100 gm	210
Amount required for a 3 m row	15 gm
Expected yield from a 3 m row	3.5 kg (bush vars.)
Expected yield from a 3 m row	5.5 kg (climbing vars.)
Life expectancy of stored seed	2 years
Approximate time between sowing and picking	8 - 12 weeks
Ease of cultivation	Easy

CALENDAR

For an early crop sow a quick-maturing variety in early May. If you want beans before the end of June you will have to use cloches. Put the cloches in position in early March and sow the seeds in the soil beneath them in early or mid April. Remove the cloches in late May.

Sow the first maincrop in May. For pods up to early October sow successively until the end of June. For a late autumn crop sow in July and cover with cloches in mid September.

Month	JAN	FEB	MAR	APR	MAY	JUN	JUL	AUG	SEP	OCT	NOV	DEC
Sowing Time												
Picking Time												

15

SOWING THE CROP

French beans will succeed in any soil provided it is neither very heavy nor acid. Lime, if necessary, in winter.

Pick a reasonably sunny spot which was not used for beans last year. Dig in autumn and add compost or well-rotted manure. Prepare the seed bed about 2 weeks before sowing — apply a general-purpose fertilizer at this time. Do not sow before the recommended date — seed will rot in cold and wet soil.

Beans sown in pots under glass in April are planted out once the danger of frost has passed.

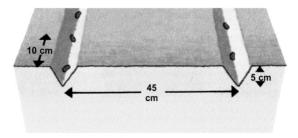

LOOKING AFTER THE CROP

Hoe the young crop regularly to keep the weeds down — protect seedlings against slugs. Support the plants with short twigs to stop them from toppling over. Use plastic netting for climbing varieties.

Spraying the flowers is not necessary to ensure that they will set properly. Moisture at the roots, however, is essential to ensure maximum pod development and a long cropping period. Water copiously and regularly in dry weather during and after the flowering period.

Mulch around the stems in June. Feed the plants with a liquid fertilizer once the pods have all been harvested. In this way a second (smaller) crop can be obtained.

HARVESTING THE CROP

Begin picking when the pods are about 10 cm long. A pod is ready if it snaps easily when bent but before bulges due to maturing beans appear along its length. Pick several times a week to prevent any pods from ripening — cropping should continue for 5 - 7 weeks. Take care not to loosen the plants when picking — hold the stems as you tug the pods, or you can play safe and use a pair of scissors.

For dried beans (haricots) leave the pods on the plant until they are straw coloured, and then hang the plants to dry. Shell the beans when the pods have begun to split — dry them on a sheet of paper for several days and then store the beans in an air-tight container.

VARIETIES

Most french (dwarf) beans are 30 - 45 cm high compact bushes, but a few are 2 m high climbers which need support.

GREEN varieties

The most popular group with scores of old and new varieties. The established ones are usually flat-podded — flat, rather wide and liable to be stringy when mature. The round pencil-podded types are stringless.

BLUE LAKE The most popular climbing variety — the pencil pods have white seeds. Good for freezing.

CROPPER TEEPEE The pencil pods are large with white seeds. A heavy cropper with good disease resistance.

DELINEL A pencil-podded bean grown for its high yields, long picking season and unique flavour.

HUNTER A high-yielding climber which is widely available — the flat pods are long, wide and straight.

MASTERPIECE STRINGLESS Good for early sowing — the flat pods are long and slim. An old favourite.

SAFARI Quick-maturing variety with narrow pencil pods. Pods are held high off the ground.

TENDERGREEN Fleshy pencil pods — early, prolific and stringless. Suitable for growing in a pot.

THE PRINCE Long fleshy flat pods renowned for their flavour and freezing qualities. Very popular.

COLOURED varieties

Apart from the novelty value there is a practical advantage — the pods can be easily seen at picking time.

KINGHORN WAX A stringless yellow flat-podded bean. The creamy yellow flesh is renowned for its flavour.

PURPLE QUEEN One of the best purple pencil pods. Beans turn dark green when cooked.

The Prince   *Safari*   *Kinghorn Wax*

BEAN, RUNNER

The long flat pods of this vegetable are Britain's favourite home-grown beans. Decorative in flower and highly productive, but not as easy as some books suggest. Thorough ground preparation is necessary in winter and so are strong supports. Weekly watering will be required in dry weather once the pods have begun to form and picking every other day in late summer is essential. Let a few pods reach maturity and the flower-producing mechanism switches off.

Expected germination time	7 - 14 days
Approximate number per 100 gm	100
Amount required for a 3 m double row	30 gm
Expected yield from a 3 m double row	25 kg
Life expectancy of stored seed	2 years
Approximate time between sowing and picking	12 - 14 weeks
Ease of cultivation	Not really easy

CALENDAR

The standard method is to sow seeds outdoors when the danger of frost has passed — late May in the south or early June in the north. Sow a few extra seeds to provide transplants to fill any gaps. A second sowing in June in mild areas will provide an October crop.

Runner beans are sometimes grown by planting out seedlings when there is no longer a risk of frosty nights. These seedlings are either shop-bought or raised at home by sowing seeds under glass in late April. This method is recommended for the colder parts of the country.

Month	JAN	FEB	MAR	APR	MAY	JUN	JUL	AUG	SEP	OCT	NOV	DEC
Sowing Time (outdoors)					▓							
Sowing Time (indoors)				⬚	⬚							
Picking Time								▓		▓		

SOWING THE CROP

Results will be disappointing in starved, badly-drained soil. Acid land is also to be avoided — lime, if necessary, in late winter.

Choose a sheltered spot where the dense shade cast by the foliage will not affect nearby plants. Dig in autumn and add an abundant supply of compost or well-rotted manure. Rake in a general-purpose fertilizer about 2 weeks before sowing or planting.

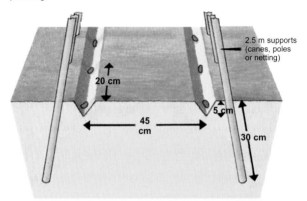

The usual method of support is to have a double line of inwardly-sloping and crossed poles with a horizontal holding bar tied along the ridge. Alternatively use a wigwam of poles, planting a seed at the base of each upright. Netting or string can be stretched between uprights, but it is difficult to keep such a structure rigid.

LOOKING AFTER THE CROP

Tie the young plants loosely to the supports, after which they will climb naturally. Protect from slugs.

Hoe regularly — mulching will help to conserve moisture. Water regularly in dry weather once pods have formed. Don't bother misting to help pollination — it isn't necessary. Liquid feed occasionally during the cropping season.

Remove the tips once the plants have reached the tops of the supports. At the end of the season dig in the stems and roots.

HARVESTING THE CROP

Pick regularly once the pods have reached 15 - 20 cm but before the beans inside have started to swell. Removing pods at this stage should ensure that cropping can continue for at least 8 weeks. This calls for picking every couple of days so that none of the pods has the chance to ripen fully.

VARIETIES

STICK varieties

Stick or standard varieties grow 2.5 - 3 m high and bear pods which can reach 25 - 50 cm. The usual flower colour is red — the white, pink and bicoloured varieties are self-pollinating. Runner beans are sometimes grown as bushy plants by picking off the tips when the stems are 30 cm high — side shoots are removed weekly. Stems are supported by twigs.

ENORMA A popular choice for the garden show — an improved form of Prizewinner. Above average flavour.

LADY DI Slender stringless pods up to 30 cm long — good for kitchen use and also for the show bench.

MERGOLES White flowers, white seeds and stringless pods. Desiree is a similar variety.

PAINTED LADY The white-faced flowers have bright red lips. The pods are relatively short. Less vigorous than most.

POLESTAR A popular stringless variety with red flowers. Yields are heavy and there is a long cropping season.

RED RUM The foliage is sparse but the pods are not. A very early crop of 20 cm long beans is obtained.

SCARLET EMPEROR An all-round performer — long and straight dark green pods. Earlier than most varieties.

STREAMLINE An old favourite, dependable and still popular as an exhibition variety.

WHITE LADY A white-flowered stringless variety with long pods. Sets well in hot weather.

DWARF varieties

A few true dwarfs are available — 30 - 45 cm high with 20 cm long pods. Grow 15 cm apart in 60 cm wide rows.

HESTIA A modern bicoloured (red/white) dwarf which is replacing the old favourite Hammond's Dwarf Scarlet.

PICKWICK A stringless variety — strong and bushy needing little or no support. Red flowers.

Enorma *White Lady* *Pickwick*

BEET, LEAF

A good alternative for people who find spinach hard to grow. Both types of leaf beet (swiss chard and spinach beet) are very easy, succeeding in ordinary soils and not bolting in dry weather. Pick from July to the following June by covering the plants in winter.

Expected germination time	10 - 14 days
Approximate number per 10 gm	700
Expected yield from a 3 m row	3 kg
Life expectancy of stored seed	3 years
Approximate time between sowing and picking	12 weeks
Ease of cultivation	Easy

CALENDAR

Month	JAN	FEB	MAR	APR	MAY	JUN	JUL	AUG	SEP	OCT	NOV	DEC
Sowing Time												
Picking Time												

SOWING THE CROP

Any reasonable soil in sun or light shade will do — the ideal is rich, well-manured loam. Dig the soil in autumn and incorporate a liberal amount of compost or well-rotted manure. Rake in a general-purpose fertilizer 2 weeks before sowing.

Leaf beet 'seed' is really a fruit — each corky cluster contains several true seeds.

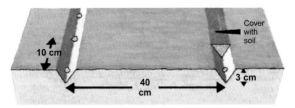

10 cm

40 cm

Cover with soil

3 cm

LOOKING AFTER THE CROP

Thin the seedlings to 30 cm apart when they are large enough to handle. Hoe regularly to keep the ground weed-free. Bolting is unlikely, but remove any flower-heads which may appear.

Water at fortnightly intervals when the weather is dry. Mulching will help to conserve moisture.

Cover the plants with cloches or straw in late autumn to ensure winter, spring and early summer cropping.

HARVESTING THE CROP

Pull off outer leaves when they are large enough for kitchen use — do not wait until they have reached their maximum size. Harvest carefully and regularly — do not disturb the roots. Leave the central foliage to develop for later pickings.

VARIETIES

RHUBARB CHARD Other name: Ruby chard. It is similar in growth habit to swiss chard but the stalks are red and thinner. More colourful for the border, but the flavour is inferior to the white type.

SPINACH BEET Other name: Perpetual spinach. Similar to spinach in appearance but the leaves are larger, darker and fleshier. Pick when small — do not use old leaves.

SWISS CHARD Other names: Silver chard, seakale beet. Grows 45 cm high with distinctive foliage. The leaf stalks and veins are white — attractive enough for the flower border. Varieties include Lucullus and White Silver 2.

Rhubarb Chard

Swiss Chard

BEETROOT

This popular vegetable is easy to grow — it is rather slow to start but growth is rapid once the seedlings are through. The secret of success is to avoid any check to growth and to pull the roots before they become large and woody. This calls for sowing short rows at monthly intervals and watering in dry weather. Home-grown beetroot can be eaten all year round. It is pulled for use fresh from the garden from June to late autumn and then it is taken from store until March. The gap between March and June is bridged by using beets from last year's crop which have been pickled or frozen.

Expected germination time	10 - 14 days
Approximate number per 10 gm	700
Expected yield from a 3 m row	4 kg (globe vars.)
Expected yield from a 3 m row	8 kg (long vars.)
Approximate time between sowing and lifting	11 weeks (globe vars.)
Approximate time between sowing and lifting	16 weeks (long vars.)
Ease of cultivation	Easy

CALENDAR

Sow a bolt-resistant variety under cloches or in a frame in early March for a late May - early June crop.

The main sowing period begins outdoors in mid April. A second sowing of globe varieties in mid May will provide a regular supply of tender roots.

Sow in late May or June for winter storage — the roots from earlier sowings may be too coarse at lifting time in October. Detroit Little Ball can be sown in July for a late autumn crop.

Month	JAN	FEB	MAR	APR	MAY	JUN	JUL	AUG	SEP	OCT	NOV	DEC
Sowing Time												
Lifting Time												

SOWING THE CROP

Any reasonable soil can produce good crops but you will need deep and sandy land for prize-winning long roots. Choose a sunny spot and dig in late autumn or winter — add well-rotted compost if the organic content is low. Apply lime if the soil is acid. Prepare the seed bed in spring — rake in a general-purpose fertilizer 2 - 3 weeks before sowing.

Beetroot 'seed' is really a fruit, consisting of a corky cluster containing several true seeds — varieties beginning with Mo-have seed clusters with just one seed.

Soak beetroot seed in warm water overnight to speed up germination.

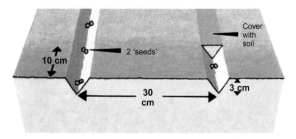

LOOKING AFTER THE CROP

Thin out when the seedlings are about 3 cm high — leave a single plant at each station. Do not use the thinnings as transplants. Protection from birds may be necessary.

Hoe to keep the land weed-free — be careful not to touch the roots. Dryness leads to woodiness and a sudden return to wet conditions leads to splitting. To avoid problems water every fortnight during dry spells. Mulching helps to conserve moisture.

Pull up alternate plants when the roots have reached golf-ball size — use for cooking. Leave the remainder to develop to an acceptably large but not maximum size.

HARVESTING THE CROP

Pull up globe varieties as needed — they should be no larger than cricket balls. There should be no white rings when the root is cut in half.

Lift roots grown for storage in October. Cylindrical and long varieties should be carefully prised out of the soil with a fork. Shake off the soil and discard damaged specimens. Place the roots between layers of dry peat in a stout box and store in a shed. The crop will keep until March.

After a beetroot has been lifted for immediate use in the kitchen or for storage the foliage should be twisted off to leave a 5 cm crown of stalks. Cutting off the leaves with a knife will result in bleeding.

VARIETIES

GLOBE varieties

Other names: Round or ball varieties. By far the most popular group — generally quick-maturing and the ones chosen to provide roots for summer cooking. With monogerm varieties reduce spacing between seeds to 5 cm.

BOLTARDY The usual choice for early sowing — widely available. Bolt-resistant. Smooth-skinned with dark red flesh.

BURPEE'S GOLDEN Orange skin, yellow flesh. Flavour is outstanding — tops can be cooked as 'greens'.

DETROIT 2 - CRIMSON GLOBE A popular Detroit variety which is recommended for successional sowing.

DETROIT 2 - LITTLE BALL A good choice for late sowing — 'baby' beets are excellent for pickling.

MONOGRAM One of the monogerm (no thinning) varieties — others include Modella, Modeda and Moneta.

PABLO One of the newer hybrids for cooking or the show bench. Uniform smooth roots with good disease resistance.

RED ACE An excellent kitchen and exhibition variety — dark red flesh. Better than most in dry weather.

CYLINDRICAL varieties

Other names: Tankard or intermediate varieties. They are a good choice if growing for winter storage.

CYLINDRA The most popular cylindrical variety. Oval with excellent keeping qualities. Dark red flesh.

FORONO An improved version of the old favourite Formanova. Ideal family size — 15 - 20 cm long and 5 cm across.

LONG varieties

Other name: Tapered varieties. Not really suitable for kitchen use, but they are firm favourites with exhibitors.

CHELTENHAM GREEN TOP By far the most popular long variety, but nowadays seed may not be easy to find.

Red Ace *Forono* *Cheltenham Green Top*

BROCCOLI

Unlike cauliflowers nearly all varieties of broccoli have sprouting heads which are harvested in a cut-and-come-again way. The seeds are sown in spring and planted out in summer — the calabrese (green) varieties are harvested in autumn and both the purple and white ones are cut in the following spring. These purple and white varieties are extremely useful as they are both hardy and high-yielding with produce which fills the gap left between the sprouts and the spring cabbages. New and exciting varieties continue to appear in the catalogues.

Expected germination time	7 - 12 days
Approximate number per 10 gm	3000
Expected yield per plant	700 gm
Life expectancy of stored seed	4 years
Approximate time between sowing and cutting	12 weeks (calabrese vars.)
Approximate time between sowing and cutting	44 weeks (purple and white vars.)
Ease of cultivation	Easier than cauliflower

CALENDAR

The date you can start cutting depends on the variety and the weather. Early Purple Sprouting will be ready for its first picking in January if the winter is mild, but mid spring is the peak harvesting time for the purple and white varieties.

The calabrese varieties will be ready for cutting in autumn — choose an early variety such as Express Corona if you want to begin in August. Cropping of late varieties will extend into winter if prolonged frosts are absent.

Month	JAN	FEB	MAR	APR	MAY	JUN	JUL	AUG	SEP	OCT	NOV	DEC
Sowing Time												
Planting Time												
Cutting Time		EARLY vars.		LATE vars.					GREEN vars.			

SOWING & PLANTING THE CROP

For best results the ground should be firm and rich in organic matter. Choose a reasonably sunny site for the place where the plants will grow to maturity. Dig in autumn — work in plenty of well-rotted manure or compost if the soil is poor. Lime, if necessary, in winter.

In spring apply a general-purpose fertilizer. Do not fork over the surface before planting the seedlings — tread down gently, rake lightly and remove surface rubbish.

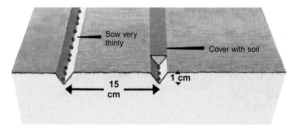

In the seed bed thin the seedlings to about 8 cm apart — they are ready for transplanting when 8 - 10 cm high. Water the rows the day before moving the transplants to their permanent quarters. Plant firmly, setting the plants about 3 cm deeper than they were growing in the seed bed. Leave 45 cm between purple or white sprouting plants — 30 cm between calabrese. Water after planting.

LOOKING AFTER THE CROP

In spring hoe regularly and protect the young plants against birds. Summer care consists of watering in dry weather and mulching to conserve moisture. Watch for pests — see The Pocket Garden Troubles Expert.

As winter approaches draw up soil around the stems and stake the plants if necessary. Always firm the stems if they are loosened by wind or frost. Pigeons can be a menace at this time of year — netting may be necessary.

HARVESTING THE CROP

Cut the flower shoots ('spears') when they are well-formed but before the small flower buds have opened. When in flower the spears are woody and tasteless.

Cut or snap off the central spear first — in a few varieties this will be a cauliflower-like head. Side shoots will be produced and these should be picked regularly.

Spears suitable for kitchen use are generally about 10 - 15 cm long, and cropping should continue for about 6 weeks. Production will stop at an earlier stage if you let any of the spears reach the flowering stage.

VARIETIES

PURPLE SPROUTING varieties

The hardiest and most popular broccoli — it will grow in cold heavy soil where little else can overwinter.

CLARET The first of the modern F_1 hybrids — vigorous, uniform and higher-than-normal yields.

EARLY PURPLE SPROUTING The favourite variety which is ready for cutting in March or April. Long cropping season.

LATE PURPLE SPROUTING Tall and robust plants — the spears are not ready for picking until April.

WHITE SPROUTING varieties

Small cauliflower-like spears are produced — less popular than the purple-sprouting varieties.

EARLY WHITE SPROUTING The one to grow if you want to start cutting spears in March.

LATE WHITE SPROUTING Spears appear in April and early May — White Star is a named variety.

CALABRESE varieties

The delicately-flavoured spears appear in autumn — one or two produce a single large head.

CORVET A succession of secondary spears appears after the removal of the large primary head.

EXPRESS CORONA Cropping starts in August — side shoots develop after the central head has been removed.

ROMANESCO Lime green spears — texture is soft and the flavour is outstanding. Heads appear in November.

TRIXIE Resistance to club root is its main feature. Spears are short and thick — matures early.

PERENNIAL variety

This tall-growing vegetable produces about 8 pale green small heads every spring — set the plants 1 m apart.

Early Purple Sprouting

Express Corona

BRUSSELS SPROUT

To avoid disappointment you will need to choose one of the modern F₁ hybrids, follow the instructions on these pages and then take care not to overcook them. Two common causes of open sprouts are loose soil and incorrect planting. You can begin picking in September and finish in March if you grow both early and late varieties — each plant should remain productive for about 8 weeks. Brussels sprouts do need adequate space — 80 cm is the usual planting distance, but Peer Gynt can be grown at 50 cm intervals for a crop of small sprouts.

Expected germination time	7 - 12 days
Approximate number per 10 gm	3000
Expected yield per plant	1 kg
Life expectancy of stored seed	4 years
Approximate time between sowing and picking	28 weeks (early vars.)
Approximate time between sowing and picking	36 weeks (late vars.)
Ease of cultivation	Not difficult

CALENDAR

For sprouts during October and November you should sow an early variety outdoors in mid March and then plant them out in mid May. If you want to have plants ready for picking in September it will be necessary to sow the seeds under cloches in early March and plant out in early May.

For a late crop which will produce sprouts between December and March, choose a late variety and sow the seeds in April. Plant out in June.

Month	JAN	FEB	MAR	APR	MAY	JUN	JUL	AUG	SEP	OCT	NOV	DEC
Sowing Time			▓	▓								
Planting Time					▓	▓						
Picking Time	▓	▓	▓						▓	▓	▓	▓

SOWING & PLANTING THE CROP

Pick a sheltered and reasonably sunny spot for the place where the plants will grow to maturity. Dig in autumn — work in plenty of compost or well-rotted manure if the soil is poor. The ground must not be acid — lime, if necessary, in winter.

In spring apply a general-purpose fertilizer. Brussels sprouts need firm soil — do not fork over the surface before planting the seedlings. Tread down gently, rake lightly and remove the surface rubbish.

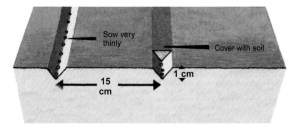

In the seed bed thin the seedlings to about 8 cm apart — they are ready for transplanting when about 15 cm high. Water the rows the day before moving to their permanent quarters. Plant firmly, setting the seedlings with their lowest leaves just above the surface. Leave about 80 cm between the plants and water after planting.

LOOKING AFTER THE CROP

Protect the seedlings from birds. Hoe regularly and water the young plants in dry weather. Brussels sprouts respond remarkably well to feeding in early summer. Watch out for pests — see The Pocket Garden Troubles Expert.

As autumn approaches earth up around the stems and stake tall varieties. The traditional practice of removing the tops off the plants in order to hasten maturity is no longer recommended.

HARVESTING THE CROP

Begin harvesting when the sprouts ('buttons') at the base of the stem have reached the size of a walnut and are still tightly closed. Snap them off with a sharp downward tug or cut them off with a sharp knife.

Work steadily up the stem at each picking session, removing yellowed leaves and any open ('blown') sprouts as you go. Remember to remove only a few sprouts at any one time from each individual stem. The secret of success is to pick them while they still feel hard and to boil them briskly for a short time.

Dig up and dispose of the stems when all the sprouts have gone.

VARIETIES

F₁ HYBRID varieties

The popularity of the modern F_1 hybrids is due to the compact growth habit of most of them and the large number of uniform-sized sprouts. Tend to mature all at the same time.

BRAVEHEART The main claim to fame of this variety is its excellent flavour after Christmas.

CASCADE Dark green sprouts can be harvested over a long period. One of the high-yielding varieties.

CITADEL Later than Peer Gynt — reaches its peak on Christmas Day. Medium-sized — recommended for freezing.

MAXIMUS Successional sowing will give you sprouts from September until the New Year. Good disease resistance.

PEER GYNT The one you will find in all the catalogues. Medium-sized sprouts from September to December.

TOPLINE A tall variety which produces large sprouts for picking in November and December.

TRAFALGAR Noted for its sweet flavour — the attractive tight buttons make it a good choice for exhibiting.

STANDARD varieties

These old favourites have been overtaken by the F_1 hybrids — the sprouts are not uniform and they blow quite quickly. But here you will find the largest sprouts and perhaps the best flavours.

BEDFORD FILLBASKET One of the Bedford varieties — the one to choose for the heaviest yields and the largest sprouts.

EVESHAM SPECIAL Large sprouts for picking from October to December. Does well in exposed sites.

ROODNERF A group of varieties which keep their sprouts without blowing for longer than other standard varieties.

RUBINE The red sprout — serve raw in salad or boil like any other variety.

Peer Gynt

Trafalgar

Bedford Fillbasket

CABBAGE

You can have cabbages from the garden all year round. By choosing the proper varieties, having enough land to spare and then sowing and transplanting at the right time you can have a non-stop supply. This quest for year-round cabbage is not for everyone, but even if you grow just one variety you should avoid sowing too many at one time — just a small row every few weeks is the proper way. Nearly all of the varieties fall neatly into one of the three major groups — spring, summer or winter cabbage. The season refers to the time of harvesting and not planting, and there are a few varieties such as Winnigstadt which are ready for cutting in autumn. You will find these autumn ones listed in the catalogues as either summer or winter varieties. You can cut-and-come-again with spring and summer cabbages, and for something different you can try one of the red or chinese varieties.

Expected germination time	7 - 12 days
Approximate number per 10 gm	3000
Expected yield per plant	300 gm - 1.5 kg
Approximate time between sowing and cutting	35 weeks (spring vars.)
Approximate time between sowing and cutting	20 - 35 weeks (summer, winter, savoy, red vars.)
Approximate time between sowing and cutting	10 weeks (chinese vars.)
Ease of cultivation	Not difficult

TYPES

SPRING

SUMMER

WINTER

SAVOY

RED

CHINESE

SOWING & PLANTING THE CROP

Pick a reasonably sunny spot for the place where the plants are to grow. Dig in autumn — work in plenty of compost or well-rotted manure if the soil is poor. The ground must not be acid — lime, if necessary, in winter.

About a week before planting apply a general-purpose fertilizer for all types except spring cabbage — this group needs to be grown slowly in a sheltered spot. Cabbages need firm soil — do not fork over the surface. Tread down gently, rake lightly and remove the surface rubbish.

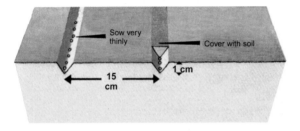

In the seed bed thin the seedlings to about 8 cm apart — they are ready for transplanting when they have 5 or 6 leaves. Water the rows the day before moving to their permanent quarters. Plant firmly and water in thoroughly.

Leave 30 cm between the plants for compact varieties — allow 45 cm either way if it is a large-headed variety. With spring cabbage leave only 10 cm between plants in rows 30 cm apart — the thinnings will provide spring greens in March.

LOOKING AFTER THE CROP

Protect the seedlings from birds. Hoe regularly and water young plants in dry weather. Apply a liquid feed as the heads begin to mature. In autumn earth-up the stems of spring cabbage. During winter firm down any plants loosened by wind or frost.

HARVESTING THE CROP

Thin out the spring cabbage rows in March and leave the remaining ones to heart up for cutting in April or May.

Cut the stems with a sharp knife close to ground level. With spring and summer cabbage cut a 1 cm deep cross into the stumps — a secondary crop of small cabbages will appear from the cut surfaces.

Cabbages are usually cut for immediate use. Both red and winter white cabbages can be cut in November and stored for winter use. Remove outer leaves and place in straw-lined boxes. The crop should keep until March.

VARIETIES

SPRING cabbages

Planted in autumn for spring greens in early spring and for mature heads later in the season. Generally conical.

APRIL Compact, small to medium-sized heads. Good for close planting. Dark green — early maturing.

DURHAM EARLY Popular, especially as a source of spring greens. Dark green medium-sized heads — early maturing.

OFFENHAM 2 - FLOWER OF SPRING This is the one to grow if you want to harvest large solid heads in April - May.

PIXIE Very early — grow for spring greens or wait until the small, tightly-packed heads mature.

SPRING HERO Unique — a ball-headed spring cabbage. Stays for weeks without splitting — heads up to 1 kg.

WHEELERS IMPERIAL Dark green compact heads for harvesting in April and May. Flavour is rated as excellent.

Month	JAN	FEB	MAR	APR	MAY	JUN	JUL	AUG	SEP	OCT	NOV	DEC
Sowing Time							▓	░				
Planting Time									▓	░		
Cutting Time			░	▓	▓							

RED cabbages

Grow it like a summer cabbage, cutting in early autumn for cooking or late autumn for storing over winter.

RED DRUMHEAD The most popular variety. Compact plants produce solid, dark red heads for cooking and pickling.

RUBY BALL An F_1 hybrid which is claimed to be better than the older varieties. Start cutting in late summer.

Month	JAN	FEB	MAR	APR	MAY	JUN	JUL	AUG	SEP	OCT	NOV	DEC
Sowing Time			░	▓								
Planting Time				░	▓							
Cutting Time									▓	░		

April

Ruby Ball

SUMMER cabbages

Ready for cutting in summer or autumn. Sow outdoors in April, transplant in May and cut in August or September. For June cabbages sow an early variety under cloches in late February/ early March and transplant in April. Usually ball-headed.

GREYHOUND An old favourite — the compact, pointed heads mature quickly. A good choice for early sowing.

HISPI A modern variety with the conical shape of Greyhound, but is claimed to mature even more quickly.

PRIMO (GOLDEN ACRE) The most popular ball-headed summer cabbage. Compact and firm.

STONEHEAD An F_1 hybrid which produces heavy round heads — stands well without splitting.

WINNIGSTADT The large, pointed heads of this old favourite are ready for cutting in September or October.

Month	JAN	FEB	MAR	APR	MAY	JUN	JUL	AUG	SEP	OCT	NOV	DEC
Sowing Time		▨	▨	■	■							
Planting Time					■	■						
Cutting Time							░	■	■	░		

CHINESE cabbages

Tall and cylindrical — they look more like a cos lettuce than a cabbage. Cultivation is also uncabbage-like — sow at 10 cm spacings in drills 30 cm apart and thin to 30 cm. Do not transplant — water in dry weather.

JADE PAGODA Different from most other varieties — the heads are tall and thin. Eat cooked or raw in salads.

Month	JAN	FEB	MAR	APR	MAY	JUN	JUL	AUG	SEP	OCT	NOV	DEC
Sowing Time							░	■				
Cutting Time										■	░	

Stonehead

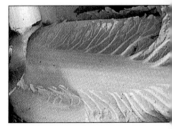

Jade Pagoda

WINTER cabbages

Green varieties are cooked immediately after cutting, but the white varieties can be stored for months. Sow in May, transplant in July and cut from November onwards.

CELTIC An F$_1$ hybrid of a savoy and winter white cabbage. Ball-headed — stands for months without splitting.

CHRISTMAS DRUMHEAD This dwarf variety is earlier than most — cut the blue-green heads from late October.

HOLLAND WINTER WHITE The traditional white cabbage for coleslaw and storage — keeps for many weeks.

JANUARY KING Drum-headed savoy type — you can tell it by its red-tinged leaves. Harvest in December and January.

TUNDRA The heads are ready in November but will still be suitable for cutting in March. Unrivalled winter hardiness.

Month	JAN	FEB	MAR	APR	MAY	JUN	JUL	AUG	SEP	OCT	NOV	DEC
Sowing Time					██							
Planting Time							██					
Cutting Time	██	██	██								██	██

SAVOY cabbages

Easily recognised by their crisp and puckered green leaves. They are grown in the same way as winter cabbages.

COLORSA Something different — a savoy/red cabbage hybrid. Compact heads with red-veined leaves.

ORMSKIRK LATE A popular variety which does not reach cutting size until February or March. Large, dark green heads.

SAVOY KING Vigorous variety with large, solid heads. The leaves are pale green and the flavour is good.

Month	JAN	FEB	MAR	APR	MAY	JUN	JUL	AUG	SEP	OCT	NOV	DEC
Sowing Time				██	██							
Planting Time							██					
Cutting Time	██	██	██								██	██

Celtic

Ormskirk Late

CAPSICUM

Sweet pepper varieties are widely used in salads and cooking, but their fiery relatives (chilli peppers) are much less popular. Capsicum is related to the tomato and requires similar growing conditions — greenhouse cultivation in most areas but they can be grown outdoors in mild regions.

Expected germination time	14 - 21 days
Expected yield per plant	6 - 10 fruits
Life expectancy of stored seed	5 years
Approximate time between sowing and picking	18 weeks
Ease of cultivation	Difficult outdoors

CALENDAR

Month	JAN	FEB	MAR	APR	MAY	JUN	JUL	AUG	SEP	OCT	NOV	DEC
Sowing & Planting Time (outdoor crop)			▮		✦							
Sowing & Planting Time (greenhouse crop)		▮▮	✦✦									
Picking Time								▨	▨			

SOWING & PLANTING THE CROP

Raise seedlings under glass at 15° - 20°C. Sow 2 seeds in a compost-filled pot — remove weaker seedling. Harden off before planting outdoors.

For outdoor cultivation well-drained fertile soil in a sunny sheltered location is necessary. Add a general-purpose fertilizer before planting.

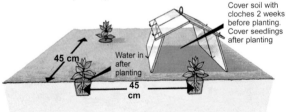

Cover soil with cloches 2 weeks before planting. Cover seedlings after planting

45 cm

Water in after planting

45 cm

Under glass grow in pots filled with compost — pot on to 5 litre size. Alternatively plant in growing bags — 3 per bag.

LOOKING AFTER THE CROP

It will be necessary to repot in several stages until the plants are ready to be moved to their permanent site.

The plants should be misted regularly to keep down attacks by red spider mite and to encourage fruit set. Some form of support is necessary — attach the stems to stakes or to horizontal wires. Plants will grow about 1 m tall under glass or 60 cm outdoors — pinching out the growing tips is not recommended.

Water regularly but do not keep the compost sodden in bags or pots. Add a potassium-rich feed such as tomato fertilizer with each watering once the fruits have begun to swell.

HARVESTING THE CROP

Pick the first fruits when they are green, swollen and glossy. A mature green pepper will turn red in about 3 weeks under glass.

VARIETIES

CALIFORNIA WONDER The block-shaped red and green fruits have a mild flavour — a reliable variety.

CAYENNE A variety for the lovers of hot peppers. Long fruits ripen to red in August or September.

GYPSY An F_1 hybrid which is claimed to be an improvement on the old favourite Canape. Early maturing.

REDSKIN A dwarf variety for the sheltered patio. Pointed fruits turn dark red when mature.

RUBY KING & GOLDEN QUEEN A Victorian variety which produces red and orange block-shaped fruits in late summer.

Gypsy

Redskin

CARROT

The way to grow long and straight-sided carrots for the local show is to create a deep hole, shaped like a giant ice cream cone, with a crowbar. Fill this hole with potting compost and sow 3 seeds of a long-rooted exhibition variety. Thin the seedlings to leave the strongest one and then feed and water regularly. Growing carrots for the kitchen is much easier — choose one of the shorter varieties and follow the instructions on these two pages. Delay the sowing of maincrop carrots until June if carrot fly is known to be a menace.

Expected germination time	17 days
Approximate number of seeds per 10 gm	7000
Expected yield from a 3 m row	3.5 kg (early vars.)
Expected yield from a 3 m row	4.5 kg (maincrop vars.)
Life expectancy of stored seed	4 years
Approximate time between sowing and lifting	12 weeks (early vars.)
Approximate time between sowing and lifting	16 weeks (maincrop vars.)
Ease of cultivation	Not difficult

CALENDAR

For a very early crop which will be ready in June, sow a short-rooted variety under cloches or in a cold frame in early March. For an early crop which will be ready in July, sow a short-rooted variety in a sheltered spot in late March or April.

For maincrop carrots sow intermediate- or long-rooted varieties between mid April and early June for lifting in September and October. For a crop of tender carrots in November and December, sow a short-rooted variety in August and cover with cloches from October.

Month	JAN	FEB	MAR	APR	MAY	JUN	JUL	AUG	SEP	OCT	NOV	DEC
Sowing Time			✲	█	█	█	░	█				
Lifting Time						█	█	█	█	█		

SOWING THE CROP

Choose a short-rooted variety if your soil is clayey or stony. If the land has been manured during the past year don't use it for growing carrots. If you want to grow a long-rooted variety you will need soil which is deep, fertile and rather sandy.

Pick a sunny spot. Dig in autumn — do not add manure or compost. Prepare the seed bed 1 or 2 weeks before sowing — rake a general-purpose fertilizer into the surface.

Mix the seed with sand which will help you to avoid sowing too thickly. Better still, sow pelleted seed 2 cm apart.

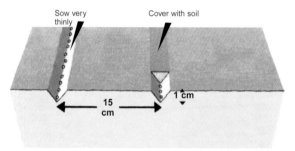

LOOKING AFTER THE CROP

Thin out the seedlings when they are large enough to handle — the plants should be 5 - 8 cm apart. Take care when thinning or the root-ruining carrot fly will be attracted by the smell of the bruised leaves. This calls for watering if the soil is dry and working in the evening. Firm the soil around the remaining plants and bury the thinnings.

Pull out or hoe any weeds between the seedlings, but hoeing around established plants is not recommended. The leaf cover provided by the densely-packed plants should keep down annual weeds — others can be removed by hand.

Water during periods of dry weather to keep the ground damp — a downpour on dry soil can lead to splitting of the roots.

HARVESTING THE CROP

Pull up small carrots as required from June onwards. Ease out with a fork if the soil is hard.

Harvest maincrop carrots in October for storage. Use a fork to lift the roots and then remove the surface dirt. Damaged roots should be used for cooking or thrown away — only sound carrots should be stored.

Cut off the leaves to about 1 cm above the crowns and then place the roots between layers of dry sand or peat in a stout box. Do not let the carrots touch each other — store in a dry shed and look at them occasionally so that any rotten roots can be removed. The carrots should keep until March.

VARIETIES

SHORT-ROOTED varieties

These golf-ball round or finger long carrots are the first to be sown for an early crop. Sow every 2 - 3 weeks from early spring to July.

AMSTERDAM FORCING One of the earliest — grow in the open or under cloches. Cylindrical and blunt (stump) ended.

EARLY NANTES 2 Roots are longer and more tapered than Amsterdam Forcing, but similar in other ways.

EARLY SCARLET HORN A reliable early variety with tapered roots — recommended for sowing under cloches in March.

PARMEX A globe-shaped early variety — a good choice for shallow soils and small plots.

INTERMEDIATE-ROOTED varieties

The best all-rounders for the average garden — usually sown later than the short-rooted varieties.

AUTUMN KING The pointed roots are unusually long for this group. Lasts well when left in the ground.

BERLICUM BERJO The cylindrical roots are stump-ended. This variety stores well over winter and has a small core.

CHANTENEY RED CORED Thick and stump-ended — the flesh is deep orange and the skin is smooth. A popular choice.

FLYAWAY A 15 cm long stump-ended carrot with better resistance to carrot fly than any other variety.

INGOT The roots can reach 20 cm or more. Smooth, deep orange and sweeter than most other varieties.

LONG-ROOTED varieties

Long, tapered giants for the show bench. Choose elsewhere if your soil is not deep, rich and light.

NEW RED INTERMEDIATE One of the longest of all carrots despite its name. Good keeping qualities.

ST. VALERY The one exhibitors usually choose. The roots are long, uniform and finely tapered.

Amsterdam Forcing

Flyaway

New Red Intermediate

CAULIFLOWER

Cauliflower is not an easy vegetable to grow. It needs rich and deep soil, and during the growing season there must not be any check to growth — failure to satisfy these conditions usually leads to the production of tiny 'button' heads. Proper soil preparation, careful planting and regular watering are essential, and so is the choice of a suitable variety. There are types to produce heads at almost any time of the year, but avoid the tender Roscoff varieties which are harvested between December and April. Grow Flora Blanca for extra-large heads or Candid Charm as a baby vegetable.

Expected germination time	7 - 12 days
Approximate number of seeds per 10 gm	3000
Expected yield per plant	500 gm - 1 kg
Life expectancy of stored seed	4 years
Approximate time between sowing and cutting	18 - 24 weeks (summer and autumn vars.)
Approximate time between sowing and cutting	40 - 50 weeks (winter vars.)
Ease of cultivation	Quite difficult

CALENDAR

Summer varieties: To provide a June - July crop sow under glass in January and transplant the seedlings in late March or early April. For an August crop sow outdoors in early April and transplant in June.

Autumn varieties: Sow outdoors between mid April and mid May — transplant in late June.

Winter varieties: To provide a March - May crop sow outdoors in May and transplant in late July.

Month	JAN	FEB	MAR	APR	MAY	JUN	JUL	AUG	SEP	OCT	NOV	DEC
Sowing Time												
Planting Time												
Cutting Time		WINTER Vars.					SUMMER Vars.			AUTUMN Vars.		

42

SOWING & PLANTING THE CROP

Pick a reasonably sunny spot for the place where the plants will grow to maturity. Avoid a frost pocket for winter varieties. Dig in autumn — work in plenty of compost or well-rotted manure. Lime, if necessary, in winter.

In spring apply a general-purpose fertilizer. Cauliflowers need firm soil — do not fork over the surface before planting the seedlings. Tread down gently, rake lightly and remove the surface rubbish.

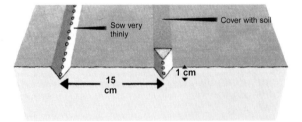

In the seed bed thin the seedlings to about 8 cm apart — they are ready for transplanting when they have 5 or 6 leaves. Water the rows the day before moving to their permanent quarters — lift carefully leaving as much soil as possible around the roots. Plant firmly, setting the seedlings at the same level as in the seed bed. Leave 60 cm between summer and autumn varieties — 75 cm between winter varieties. Water after planting.

LOOKING AFTER THE CROP

Protect the seedlings from birds and hoe regularly. The plants must never be kept short of water or very small heads will quickly form. Cauliflower is a hungry crop, so feed occasionally.

With summer varieties bend a few leaves over the developing curd to protect it from the sun.

Protect the winter crop from frost and snow by breaking a few leaves over the curd.

HARVESTING THE CROP

Begin cutting some of the cauliflowers while they are still fairly small rather than waiting for them all to mature which will produce a glut. You have waited too long if the florets have started to separate.

Cut in the morning when the heads still have dew on them — if the weather is frosty delay cutting until midday. You can keep the heads for up to 3 weeks before use — lift the plants and shake the earth off the roots before hanging them upside-down in a cool shed. Mist the curds occasionally until you are ready to use the heads.

VARIETIES

SUMMER varieties

Compact plants. Choose an early variety for June - July heads or a later-maturing one for an August crop.

ALL THE YEAR ROUND An old favourite. With successional sowing you can crop all summer and autumn.

ALPHA This early cauliflower is noted for its resistance to premature heading when conditions are not right.

SNOW CROWN An early variety with snow-white heads weighing up to 1 kg. Vigorous leaves provide protection.

SNOWBALL A popular choice for early sowing. The tight heads are not large — the large Snowball-type is Snow Crown.

AUTUMN varieties

Some types are compact, but most autumn cauliflowers produce large heads in late September - November.

BARRIER REEF Curd is well protected by broad leaves — compact heads ready for cutting in late October.

CANDID CHARM An improvement on the Australian variety Canberra — heads are ready in early October.

CASTLEGRANT A modern November-maturing variety which is now in many catalogues. Large ivory-coloured heads.

FLORA BLANCA Giant heads in late September or October — a good choice for the show bench.

PLANA Pure white heads in late September and October. Easier to grow than most varieties.

WINTER varieties

A technically incorrect name as they mature in spring. They are heading broccoli, not true cauliflowers.

PURPLE CAPE The purple heads are ready for cutting in March. Cook the young leaves as well as the curd.

WALCHEREN WINTER A Dutch variety which dominates the catalogues. There are several named strains.

Snowball

Walcheren Winter

CELERIAC

The knobbly, swollen stem-base of celeriac is about 10 - 15 cm across with a distinct celery flavour. It isn't a vegetable for everyone — you will have to raise your own seedlings as very few garden centres offer them and you will need rich and moisture-retentive soil. Regular watering in dry weather is necessary.

Expected germination time	12 - 18 days
Expected yield from a 3 m row	3 kg
Approximate time between sowing and lifting	30 - 35 weeks
Ease of cultivation	Rather difficult

CALENDAR

Month	JAN	FEB	MAR	APR	MAY	JUN	JUL	AUG	SEP	OCT	NOV	DEC
Sowing Time			▉ ▉									
Planting Time					❧ ❧							
Lifting Time												

SOWING & PLANTING THE CROP

Fertile and humus-rich soil is essential. Pick a reasonably sunny spot and dig in autumn. Incorporate as much compost or well-rotted manure as you can. About a week before planting rake in a general-purpose fertilizer.

Raise seedlings under glass in early spring. Plant 2 seeds in a compost-filled peat pot — remove the weaker seedling. Harden off before planting outdoors.

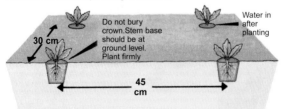

45

LOOKING AFTER THE CROP

Hoe regularly to keep down weeds and feed the plants occasionally — a mulch in early summer will conserve moisture. Remove side shoots — from midsummer onwards cut off lower leaves to expose the crown. In late September draw soil around the swollen stem-bases.

HARVESTING THE CROP

Aim for maximum size — neither flavour nor texture gets worse with age. Lifting begins in October — in most areas you can cover the roots with straw and then lift as required until early spring.

If your site is exposed and the soil is heavy, it is better to lift and store all the roots before December. Twist off the tops, cut off the roots and store in boxes filled with damp peat. Keep in a cool shed.

VARIETIES

The range of varieties is quite large — the major seed suppliers each have their own favourite, but there isn't much difference between them. In the catalogues Monarch and Mars are claimed to be improvements on the older varieties.

GIANT PRAGUE This round, turnip-shaped celeriac was once the most popular variety, but not any more.

MARS A modern variety. Large and round — an improvement on the old favourite Giant Prague.

MONARCH Smoother-skinned than most — the cream-coloured roots are large. Tolerates celery virus.

SNOW WHITE Large roots — white when cooked. A 'nutty' flavour, according to the suppliers. Widely available.

Snow White

Monarch

CELERY

Celery is a lot of effort. Trenches must be prepared and the stems must be earthed-up at intervals so that only the green tips are showing. The main purpose of this 'blanching' process is to lengthen and improve the stems and not to whiten them. You can now sow self-blanching varieties so that neither trenching nor blanching is required, but these varieties are less crisp and cannot be left in the ground once the frosts arrive. Self-blanching varieties do make celery growing easier, but not easy. Good soil plus regular watering and feeding are still necessary.

Expected germination time	12 - 18 days
Approximate number of seeds per 10 gm	25,000
Expected yield from a 3 m row	5 kg
Approximate time between sowing and lifting	40 weeks (trench vars.)
Approximate time between sowing and lifting	25 weeks (self-blanching vars.)
Ease of cultivation	Difficult

CALENDAR

Seedlings are planted out between late May and mid June. You can raise your own plants by sowing seed under heated glass between mid March and early April — make sure that the seedlings do not receive any check to growth and ensure that the plants are properly hardened off before planting out. Most people prefer to buy their seedlings — choose a reputable supplier.

Self-blanching varieties will be ready for lifting between August and October. The trench varieties are grown for winter use from October onwards.

Month	JAN	FEB	MAR	APR	MAY	JUN	JUL	AUG	SEP	OCT	NOV	DEC
Sowing Time			▪	▪								
Planting Time					✿	✿						
Lifting Time	▪	▪							▪	▪	▪	▪

47

SOWING THE CROP

A sunny site and well-prepared soil are needed. For self-blanching types dig a bed in April — add manure or compost. For trench varieties prepare a celery trench in April as shown below — allow to settle until planting time. Just before planting rake in a general-purpose fertilizer.

Sow seed under glass and harden off the seedlings before planting outdoors. Seedlings are ready for transplanting when there are 5 or 6 leaves.

Self-blanching varieties are planted 25 cm apart in a square block — not in rows.

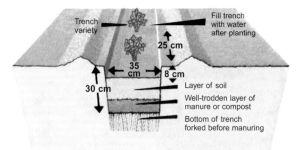

LOOKING AFTER THE CROP

Water copiously in dry weather and use a liquid feed in summer.

Blanch trench varieties in early August when about 30 cm high. Remove any side shoots, surround the stalks with news-paper or corrugated cardboard and tie loosely — then fill the trench with soil. In late August mound moist soil against the stems and in mid September complete earthing-up to produce a steep-sided mound with only the foliage tops showing. Do not let soil fall into the hearts. In frosty weather cover the tops with straw.

With self-blanching celery tuck straw between the plants which form the outside lines of the bed.

HARVESTING THE CROP

Lift self-blanching varieties as required — finish harvesting before the frosts arrive. Remove the outer plants first, using a trowel so that neighbouring plants are not damaged by the lifting process.

Lift trenching varieties according to type — white varieties up to Christmas and coloured ones in January. There is no need to wait for a sharp frost — there is little scientific evidence for the old saying that frost improves quality. Start at one end of the earthed-up row — replace soil after lifting to protect the remaining plants.

VARIETIES

TRENCH varieties

Not easy to grow as trenching and subsequent earthing-up are time-consuming jobs. Choose one if you are an exhibitor or like a challenge — otherwise pick a self-blanching variety. The white types have the best flavour but are the least hardy — grow a pink or red variety if you want a New Year crop.

GIANT PINK (pink) A hardy variety for harvesting in January or February. Crisp stalks and solid hearts.

GIANT RED (red) Outer stalks are purplish-green, turning pale red when blanched.

GIANT WHITE (white) The traditional white-stalked celery. Hopkin's Fenlander is the strain you are most likely to find.

SELF-BLANCHING varieties

These varieties need neither trenching nor earthing-up — they take some of the hard work out of celery growing. They are milder-flavoured and less stringy than the trench varieties, and are not winter hardy. There are yellow, green and pink varieties — easier to find than trench varieties.

AMERICAN GREEN (green) The basic green variety sometimes sold as Greensnap. Not easy to find.

CELEBRITY (yellow) A modern variety noted for its long stalks and bolt resistance.

GOLDEN SELF-BLANCHING (yellow) The basic yellow type, compact and ready for lifting from August.

LATHOM SELF-BLANCHING (yellow) A better choice than Golden Self-blanching — less likely to bolt.

PINK CHAMPAGNE (pink) One of the few pink self-blanching varieties. Tall colourful stems.

VICTORIA (green) A new favourite which is less demanding than the older varieties. Early-maturing.

Giant White   *Golden Self-blanching*   *American Green*

CHICORY

There are two types of chicory. The forcing varieties produce plump leafy heads ('chicons') from roots kept in the dark in winter. The other chicories are the non-forcing varieties which do not require blanching — they produce large lettuce-like heads which are ready for harvesting in autumn.

Expected germination time	7 - 14 days
Approximate number of seeds per 10 gm	7000
Expected yield from a 3 m row	3 kg
Life expectancy of stored seed	5 years
Approximate time between sowing and cutting	18 - 30 weeks
Ease of cultivation	Easy (non-forcing vars.)

CALENDAR

Month		JAN	FEB	MAR	APR	MAY	JUN	JUL	AUG	SEP	OCT	NOV	DEC
Sowing Time	FORCING vars.					█	█						
	NON-FORCING vars.						█	█					
Cutting Time	FORCING vars.	█	█	█	█								
	NON-FORCING vars.										█	█	█

SOWING THE CROP

Choose a sunny site — chicory is not fussy about soil type. Dig in autumn or winter and incorporate compost if the soil is short of humus. Prepare the seed bed a few days before sowing — rake a general-purpose fertilizer into the surface.

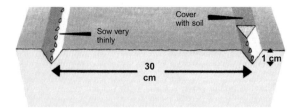

Sow very thinly

Cover with soil

30 cm

1 cm

LOOKING AFTER THE CROP

Hoe to keep down weeds — water in dry weather. Thin seedlings to 15 cm (forcing varieties) or 30 cm (non-forcing varieties).

Forcing varieties: Lift roots in November — discard fanged ones and those less than 3 cm across the crown. Cut back to 3 cm above the crown. Pack horizontally in a box of sand until required. Force a few at a time between November and March. Plant 5 in a 25 cm pot — surround each root with compost, leaving the crown exposed. Cover with an empty larger pot — block up the drainage holes. Keep at 10° - 15°C.

HARVESTING THE CROP

Forcing varieties: The chicons are ready when about 15 cm high — this will take 3 - 4 weeks. Cut just above the level of the crown. Water the compost and replace the cover — smaller secondary chicons will be produced.

Non-forcing varieties: Cut heads in late autumn — use immediately or store in a cool shed for later use.

VARIETIES

NORMATO A modern forcing variety which can be forced quite easily using the technique described above.

PALLA ROSSA Forcing or non-forcing variety. One of the red radicchios now available in supermarkets.

SNOWFLAKE One of the modern non-forcing varieties — hardier than Sugar Loaf.

SUGAR LOAF Pain de Sucre in some catalogues — the traditional non-forcing variety.

WITLOOF The traditional forcing variety. Good and reliable, but needs forcing under 20 cm of soil or peat.

Sugar Loaf

Snowflake

CUCUMBER, GREENHOUSE

The greenhouse cucumber is straight, cylindrical, smooth-skinned and shiny. These fruits reaching 45 cm or more are for the keen gardener and the exhibitor, but for many gardeners they are too much trouble. Cucumbers under glass need warmth and regular care, including regular watering and feeding, tying and stopping, protection from pests and diseases, and so on. Growing outdoor varieties involves much less work, but if you want to pick fruits in May or June for early summer salads then cultivation under glass is the only way to grow cucumbers in the garden.

Expected germination time	3 - 5 days
Expected yield per plant	25 cucumbers
Life expectancy of stored seed	6 years
Approximate time between sowing and cutting	12 weeks
Ease of cultivation	Difficult

CALENDAR

If your house is heated sow seed in late February or early March and plant out in late March or early April for a crop which will start to mature in late May or June.

Most gardeners, however, grow cucumbers in an unheated ('cold') greenhouse. Sow seed in late April and plant out in late May. Fruits appear from July onwards — pick regularly to extend the cropping season.

Month	JAN	FEB	MAR	APR	MAY	JUN	JUL	AUG	SEP	OCT	NOV	DEC
Sowing & Planting Time		▪	▪ ❦	❦ ▪	❦							
Cutting Time												

SOWING & PLANTING THE CROP

Seedlings are raised under glass — warmth (20° - 25°C) is essential. Place a single seed edgeways 1 cm deep in compost in a 7 cm pot — germination will take about 3 days. When the first leaves have expanded transfer the seedling to a 12 cm pot. Keep the compost moist.

Planting out takes place when there are about 5 leaves. Do not grow in the border — the soil soon becomes infested with soil pests and root diseases. Plant in 25 cm pots of compost (1 per pot) or in growing bags (2 per bag). Water in after planting.

LOOKING AFTER THE CROP

You will need to maintain a minimum temperature of 15°C for ordinary varieties and 20°C for all-female ones. Ideally the humidity should be higher than tomatoes require, but many people grow these vegetables together quite successfully.

Keep the compost moist but not waterlogged — little and often is the rule. Water in the morning and make slits at the bottom of the growing bags. Overwatering young plants is a common cause of failure.

The air should be kept as moist and well ventilated as the other plants in the house will allow. Spray the floor (but not the plants) with water to ensure that the air is humid.

Train each stem up a vertical wire or cane. Pinch out the growing point when the leader reaches the roof. The tip of each side shoot should be pinched out at 2 leaves beyond a female flower. Female flowers have a miniature cucumber behind them — male flowers have just a thin stalk. Pinch out the tips of flowerless side shoots when they are about 60 cm long.

It is essential that all male flowers are removed from ordinary varieties — fertilized fruits are bitter.

The nutrients in growing bags last for 4 - 6 weeks. Once the first fruits have started to swell it is necessary to feed every 2 weeks with a tomato fertilizer.

A number of fungal and bacterial diseases can attack cucumbers grown under glass — keep careful watch and follow the instructions in The Pocket Garden Troubles Expert if a problem arises.

HARVESTING THE CROP

Cut (do not pull) when the fruit has reached a reasonable size and the sides are parallel — for most varieties this will be about 30 cm. Cropping will cease if you allow cucumbers to mature and turn yellow on the plant.

VARIETIES

ORDINARY varieties

These are the traditional cucumbers of the summer salad — long, straight, smooth and dark green. Now largely replaced by the all-female varieties, they remain the first choice for the exhibitor and for some with unheated greenhouses.

BUTCHER'S DISEASE RESISTING Not as smooth-skinned as Telegraph but a heavier cropper. No longer easy to find.

TELEGRAPH An old greenhouse cucumber with several improved strains. Now the only popular ordinary variety.

ALL-FEMALE varieties

As they bear only female flowers the tiresome job of removing male flowers is unnecessary. They are more disease resistant than ordinary varieties and are more prolific, but the fruits are shorter and a higher temperature is required.

AIDAS A vigorous variety which can be grown in a cold house. Long and smooth fruits.

BIRGIT A heavy-cropping modern variety — a good one to choose if you plan to sow early.

BRUNEX A high-yielding variety for a heated or cold house — male flowers are occasionally produced.

CARMEN Outstanding resistance to powdery mildew, scab and leaf spot. Crops over a long period.

FEMSPOT Early maturing with good disease resistance, but needs more heat than most varieties.

FUTURA Suitable for growing in a cold house. Good powdery mildew resistance.

PEPINEX The first of the all-female varieties — long, straight and smooth fruits. Good flavour.

PETITA Tolerates less than ideal conditions better than most all-females — small (20 cm) fruits.

TYRIA The main feature of this strong-growing variety is its high resistance to powdery mildew.

Pepinex

Brunex

Petita

CUCUMBER, OUTDOOR

Growing long cucumbers for summer salads used to mean that you had to have a greenhouse. Outdoor or ridge cucumbers were short and dumpy with a surface covered with bumps and warts. Things have changed. There are now outdoor varieties which bear 30 cm long smooth-skinned cucumbers which are unrivalled for flavour and juiciness. There are also outdoor varieties from which indigestibility has been removed. Outdoor cucumbers used to be grown on raised beds or ridges, but nowadays they are grown on the flat. The plants have lax stems like their greenhouse cousins — these outdoor varieties are left to scramble on the ground or are supported by nets or poles.

Expected germination time	6 - 9 days
Expected yield per plant	10 cucumbers
Approximate time between sowing and cutting	12 - 14 weeks
Ease of cultivation	Not easy

CALENDAR

Seed is sown outdoors in late May or early June. In northern and midland areas cover the seedlings with cloches for a few weeks. Cropping should start in early August.

For an earlier crop sow seed under glass in late April. Plant out the seedlings in early June when the danger of frost has passed.

Month	JAN	FEB	MAR	APR	MAY	JUN	JUL	AUG	SEP	OCT	NOV	DEC
Sowing Time (outdoors)					█							
Sowing Time (indoors)				▓		⚘						
Cutting Time								▓	▓			

SOWING & PLANTING THE CROP

A sunny spot protected from strong winds is essential. The soil must be well drained and rich in humus. Prepare planting pockets as shown below about 2 weeks before sowing seed or planting seedlings.

Sow 3 seeds 2 cm deep and several cm apart at the centre of each pocket. Cover with a large jar or cloche to hasten germination. When the first true leaves have appeared thin out to leave the strongest seedling.

Alternatively you can raise the seedlings indoors, but this method is less satisfactory. Place a single seed edgeways 1 cm deep in compost in a 10 cm pot. Keep at 20° - 25°C until germination takes place — gradually harden off before planting in pockets outdoors.

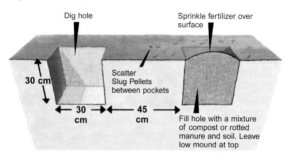

Dig hole

Sprinkle fertilizer over surface

30 cm

Scatter Slug Pellets between pockets

30 cm

45 cm

Fill hole with a mixture of compost or rotted manure and soil. Leave low mound at top

LOOKING AFTER THE CROP

Pinch out the tip when the plant has developed 6 or 7 leaves. Side shoots will develop — let them trail over the ground or train them up stout netting. Any shoots not bearing flowers should be pinched out at the 7th leaf.

Keep the soil moist — water around the plants, not over them. Place black plastic sheeting over the soil in summer before fruits develop. This cover will raise the temperature, conserve moisture, suppress weeds and protect the fruits from rotting.

Fertilization is essential — never remove the male flowers. Feed with a liquid tomato fertilizer once the first fruits have started to swell.

HARVESTING THE CROP

Cut the cucumbers before they reach their maximum size — this will encourage further fruiting. Most varieties will be 15 - 20 cm long — cut gherkins when 10 cm long.

Use a sharp knife — don't tug the fruits from the stem. The cropping period is quite short as the plants will be killed by the first frosts, but with proper care and regular picking the production of cucumbers should continue until the end of September.

VARIETIES

STANDARD RIDGE varieties

Traditional varieties are thick and knobbly. The newer F_1 hybrids are longer, smoother and more disease-resistant.

BUSH CHAMPION A bushy F_1 hybrid for pots or growing bags. Matures quickly — resistant to virus.

LONG GREEN RIDGE An improved form of the old favourite Bedfordshire Prize — a heavy cropper.

MARKETMORE Dark green with straight fruits up to 20 cm long. Good disease resistance.

ALL-FEMALE varieties

These varieties do not need fertilization so the mass of seeds associated with outdoor cucumbers is absent.

PASKA Glossy dark green fruit up to 25 cm long. Resistant to powdery mildew.

JAPANESE varieties

These include the longest and smoothest of all outdoor cucumbers. Use a stout frame of netting for support.

BURPLESS TASTY GREEN The usual choice — you will find this one in all the catalogues. Mildew resistant.

KYOTO Long, straight and smooth cucumbers to rival the ones in the greenhouse.

TOKYO SLICER Smooth and dark-skinned — shorter than Kyoto but the plants are more productive.

GHERKIN varieties

Small, warty fruits used for pickling.

VENLO PICKLING The most popular variety although others (Eureka, Conda etc) claim to be better.

APPLE varieties

Small, round and yellow fruits.

CRYSTAL APPLE The only variety you are likely to find. Easy to grow — excellent flavour.

Bush Champion

Burpless Tasty Green

Crystal Apple

ENDIVE

Endive is popular on the Continent but not in the English salad. Its flavour is more distinctive than lettuce and it has the advantage of being available between January and March from the garden. Monthly sowings can give you heads for 6 months of the year — blanching before cutting is necessary to remove bitterness.

Expected germination time	3 - 7 days
Expected yield from a 3 m row	10 - 15 heads
Approximate time between sowing and cutting	15 - 20 weeks
Ease of cultivation	Not easy

CALENDAR

Month	JAN	FEB	MAR	APR	MAY	JUN	JUL	AUG	SEP	OCT	NOV	DEC
Sowing Time			▨	▨	■	■	■	■				
Cutting Time	■	■	▨					▨	■	■	■	■

SOWING THE CROP

Choose a sunny site for summer- and autumn-sown crops — a semi-shady spot is suitable for spring-sown endive.

Dig in autumn — incorporate compost or well-rotted manure. About a week before planting apply a general-purpose fertilizer.

Sow curly-leaved varieties in March - August — broad-leaved varieties are sown in July - September for late autumn and winter use.

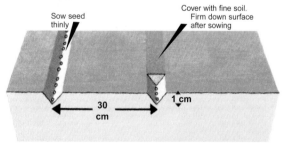

Sow seed thinly

Cover with fine soil. Firm down surface after sowing

30 cm

1 cm

LOOKING AFTER THE CROP

Thin the seedlings as soon as the first true leaves appear. Continue thinning at intervals until the plants are 25 cm (curly-leaved varieties) or 30 cm apart (broad-leaved varieties).

Hoe regularly and feed occasionally with a liquid fertilizer. Water thoroughly in dry weather or the plants will run to seed.

Begin blanching about 12 weeks after sowing. Choose a few plants and make sure the leaves are dry. Tie up the leaves loosely with raffia and cover with a plastic flower pot — block up the drainage holes. The heads will be ready in 3 weeks (summer) or 5 weeks (winter).

HARVESTING THE CROP

Sever the heads with a sharp knife when the leaves have turned creamy white.

VARIETIES

BROAD-LEAVED varieties

Lettuce-like leaves. Hardier than the curly-leaved ones — cloche-covered heads will survive over winter.

BATAVIAN GREEN May be listed as No. 52. Crisp leaves — use in cooking or as a winter salad ingredient.

JETI Large heads — growth is upright and it has a self-blanching habit.

CURLY-LEAVED varieties

Finely-divided frizzy leaves. Sow in spring and summer for a summer and autumn crop.

GREEN CURLED The most popular curly-leaved endive — sometimes listed as Moss Curled.

SALLY Reputed to be one of the easiest endives to grow — self-blanching at the centre.

Batavian Green

Sally

KALE

You will find kale in very few gardens despite its ability to provide winter and spring greens for very little effort. Unlike other members of the cabbage family it will tolerate poor soil conditions and is rarely troubled by the major enemies of the brassicas — club root, cabbage root fly and pigeons. In addition there is no vegetable more capable of withstanding sharp and prolonged frosts. Despite these good points it is generally rejected — the reason is the bitter taste of the cooked leaves. This bitterness is due to over-cooking leaves which are mature — the secret is to pick young leaves and then cook them quickly in a small amount of water. With some varieties the young shoots are used.

Expected germination time	7 - 12 days
Approximate number of seeds per 10 gm	3000
Expected yield per plant	1 kg
Life expectancy of stored seed	4 years
Approximate time between sowing and cutting	30 - 35 weeks
Ease of cultivation	Easy

CALENDAR

Sow a variety of curly-leaved kale in April if you want greens before Christmas. For later cropping sow leaf & spear or plain-leaved kale in May. The correct time for transplanting is governed by the height of the seedlings rather than the date.

Rape kale is sown in late June in a bed where it will grow to maturity — see Sowing & Planting the Crop on page 61 for details.

Month	JAN	FEB	MAR	APR	MAY	JUN	JUL	AUG	SEP	OCT	NOV	DEC
Sowing Time				▓	▓	▓						
Planting Time							▓	▓				
Cutting Time	▓	▓	▓	▓							▓	▓

SOWING & PLANTING THE CROP

Kale will grow in nearly any soil provided the drainage is satisfactory. Pick a reasonably sunny spot for the place where the plants will grow to maturity. As the seedlings are not transplanted until June or July, it is usual to use land which has been vacated by peas, early potatoes or other early summer crop. Do not dig — tread over the ground, remove any weeds and rake in a little fertilizer. Lime if the land is acid.

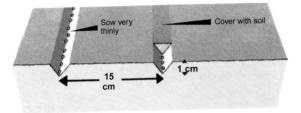

In the seed bed thin the seedlings to 8 cm apart. Transplant when they are 10 - 15 cm high. Water the rows the day before moving the transplants to their permanent quarters. Plant firmly at 45 cm intervals, with the lowest leaves just above the soil surface. Water in after planting.

Rape kale is sown where it is to grow. The seed drills should be 45 cm apart — thin seedlings in stages to 45 cm apart.

LOOKING AFTER THE CROP

Hoe regularly and tread firmly around the stems to prevent the plants from rocking in the wind. Water the plants in dry weather. Pick off yellowing leaves. Earth-up around the stems as winter approaches in order to protect the roots from frost and wind rock. Stake tall varieties if the plants are growing on an exposed site.

In early spring a crop of fresh side shoots will appear. Feed with a liquid fertilizer in March to encourage their development.

HARVESTING THE CROP

Harvest curly kale by starting at the crown of the plant from November onwards — remove a few leaves each time you pick. Use a knife or a sharp downward tug — do not collect yellowing or mature leaves for kitchen use. This initial stripping of the crown will stimulate the development of succulent side shoots.

As with all the other types of kale these side shoots are gathered between February and May, breaking them off or using a sharp knife to remove them. They should be 10 - 12 cm long — mature side shoots are not suitable for cooking.

The leaf & spear varieties also produce flower-heads ('spears') which are cut at the bud stage and cooked like broccoli.

VARIETIES

CURLY-LEAVED varieties

These 'Scotch' kales are much more popular than the other types. Each leaf has an extremely frilled and curled edge.

DARKIBOR Like Fribor a modern dark green F_1 hybrid, but this one is much taller.

DWARF GREEN CURLED The usual choice for the small plot — the 45 - 60 cm plants do not require staking.

FRIBOR An F_1 dwarf hybrid with dark green leaves, growing only 25 cm high.

REDBOR Something different — a red kale for the vegetable or flower garden. Use young leaves in salads.

TALL GREEN CURLED A tall plant with similar leaves to Dwarf Green Curled. Not easy to find.

PLAIN-LEAVED varieties

Tall kales which are generally coarser than the curly-leaved types, but they are easier to keep pest-free.

BLACK TUSCANY Long spear-shaped leaves in dark grey-green. Ornamental enough for the flower border.

THOUSAND-HEADED KALE Once widely sold by the seed houses but its place has now been taken by Black Tuscany.

RAPE KALE varieties

These kales are sown where they are to grow, providing tender shoots between March and May.

HUNGRY GAP A late cropper, like all rape kales. A robust and reliable plant — shoots are suitable for freezing.

LEAF & SPEAR variety

There is just one variety — a cross between a curly-leaved and a plain-leaved kale. A multi-use vegetable.

PENTLAND BRIG Young leaves are picked from the crown in November — leafy side shoots are gathered in early spring and later broccoli-like spears are harvested.

Fribor

Pentland Brig

KOHL RABI

Once a rarity, this member of the cabbage family has now become more familiar since its appearance in the supermarkets. The edible swollen part is not a root — it is the stem base, so this crop can succeed in shallow soils where turnips or swedes would fail.

Expected germination time	10 days
Approximate number of seeds per 10 gm	3000
Expected yield from a 3 m row	20 globes
Approximate time between sowing and lifting	8 - 12 weeks
Ease of cultivation	Easy

CALENDAR

Month	JAN	FEB	MAR	APR	MAY	JUN	JUL	AUG	SEP	OCT	NOV	DEC
Sowing Time			░	▓	▓	▓	▓					
Lifting Time						░	▓	▓	▓	▓	▓	▓

SOWING THE CROP

The ideal location is a sunny spot and sandy soil. Dig in autumn — work in compost if the soil is short of humus. Lime, if necessary, in winter. In spring apply a general-purpose fertilizer. Prepare the bed about a week later, treading down and then raking the surface.

Sow green varieties between March and June. For a late autumn or winter crop sow a purple variety in July or August.

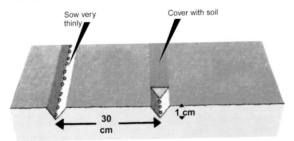

Sow very thinly

Cover with soil

30 cm

1 cm

LOOKING AFTER THE CROP

Thin the seedlings as soon as the first true leaves appear. Continue thinning at intervals until the plants are 15 cm apart. Provide protection against birds. Hoe regularly and feed occasionally if growth is slow. Soak the ground during periods of dry weather.

HARVESTING THE CROP

Pull the swollen stem bases ('globes') when they are midway in size between a golf ball and a tennis ball — do not let them grow to maturity. They are not suitable for storage — they deteriorate once out of the ground. Leave the plants growing in the garden and pull as required until December.

Grate the young globes to provide an ingredient for summer or winter salads, but it is more usual to cook before serving.

VARIETIES

AZUR STAR Purple-skinned quick-maturing variety. Good resistance to bolting — a better choice than Purple Vienna according to the suppliers.

ROWEL An F_1 hybrid which is an improvement on the old Vienna varieties. It does not become woody if allowed to grow to tennis ball size, and the flesh is claimed to be sweeter.

TRERO Another of the pale-skinned kohl rabi F_1 hybrids which is slow to go woody. Use it to give a nutty flavour to summer salads.

WHITE VIENNA Green-skinned, white-fleshed — sometimes listed as Green Vienna. Matures earlier than the purple form. Once the most popular variety, but not any more.

Azur Star

Rowel

LEEK

Leeks are the easiest member of the onion family to grow — they will withstand the hardest winter, are generally not troubled by pests and diseases, and do not demand the same level of high fertility as the onion. Not a truly easy crop, however, as they need transplanting, careful earthing-up and occupy the ground for a long time. Still, a crop which is well worth while — the harvesting season lasts for 6 months or more and the strong roots break up heavy soil. For kitchen use aim to produce 'stems' (actually shanks of rolled leaves) weighing between 250 - 500 gm.

Expected germination time	14 - 18 days
Approximate number of seeds per 10 gm	4000
Expected yield from a 3 m row	5 kg
Life expectancy of stored seed	3 years
Approximate time between sowing and lifting	30 weeks (early vars.)
Approximate time between sowing and lifting	45 weeks (late vars.)
Ease of cultivation	Not difficult

CALENDAR

For exhibiting at the autumn show sow seed under glass in late January or February and plant outdoors during April.

For kitchen use sow seed outdoors in spring when the soil is workable and warm enough for germination. Transplant the seedlings in June.

For an April crop sow seed of a late variety in June and transplant in July.

Month	JAN	FEB	MAR	APR	MAY	JUN	JUL	AUG	SEP	OCT	NOV	DEC
Sowing Time			▓	▓								
Planting Time						▓	▓					
Sowing Time (under glass)	▓	▓		☘								
Lifting Time	▓			▓	▓				▓	▓	▓	▓

SOWING & PLANTING THE CROP

Leeks will grow in any reasonable soil provided it is neither highly compacted nor badly drained. Starved soil will produce disappointing yields — add compost or well-rotted manure with the winter digging if this was not done for the previous crop.

Pick a sunny site for where the plants will grow to maturity. Leave the soil rough after digging and level the surface in spring by raking and treading. Incorporate a general-purpose fertilizer into the surface about 1 week before planting.

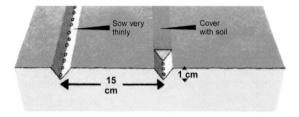

In the seed bed thin the seedlings to 4 cm apart. The young leeks are ready for transplanting when they are pencil-thick and about 20 cm high. Water the bed the day before lifting. Trim off the root ends and leaf tips, and then set out in rows 30 cm apart, leaving 15 cm between the transplants.

Make a 15 cm deep hole with a dibber, drop in the transplant and then gently fill the hole with water to settle the roots. Do not fill the hole with soil.

LOOKING AFTER THE CROP

Hoe carefully and make sure that the plants are not short of water during dry weather. Do not deliberately fill the holes with soil.

Blanching is necessary to increase the length of white stem. Gently draw dry soil around the stems when the plants are well developed. Do this in stages, increasing the height a little at a time — be careful not to allow soil to fall between the leaves. Finish earthing-up in late October.

Feeding will increase the thickness of the stems. Late feeding should be avoided on plants which are to overwinter — late August is the time to stop.

HARVESTING THE CROP

Do not aim to produce giants. These belong on the show bench and not in the kitchen — flavour reduces as size increases.

Begin lifting when the leeks are still quite small — in this way there will be a long harvesting period. Never try to wrench the plant out of the soil — lift gently with a fork.

Leeks can remain in the ground during the winter months — lift as required.

VARIETIES

EARLY varieties

Popular with exhibitors for sowing early under glass. For the kitchen there are long-stemmed leeks for autumn use.

JOLANT A vigorous grower with extra-long stems. Recommended as a baby vegetable (see page 113).

KING RICHARD A modern high-quality variety with pale green leaves. Excellent as a baby vegetable (see page 113).

LYON PRIZETAKER A favourite variety for the show bench — long, thick stems with dark green leaves. Mild flavoured.

VERINA Medium-length straight stems with dark green leaves. Good resistance to rust.

WALTON MAMMOTH One of the Autumn Mammoth strains recommended for exhibition and kitchen use. Very hardy.

MID-SEASON varieties

Winter-hardy leeks which mature during the winter months. Here you will find the most popular leek for home gardeners.

MUSSELBURGH This old variety remains the No. 1 choice. Reliable and fine flavoured, but the stems are not long.

SNOWSTAR A modern variety which is similar to Musselburgh, but is more likely to catch the judge's eye at the show.

TOLEDO A good one to pick if you want a mid-season variety with extra-long stems.

LATE varieties

Very useful for the kitchen as they mature between late January and early April when other vegetables are scarce.

WINORA A rust-resistant variety with blue-green leaves and thick, medium-length stems.

WINTER CROP This variety is often recommended for northern exposed sites as it is the hardiest of all.

YATES EMPIRE Looks like Musselburgh with thick white stems, but will stand in the ground until April.

Lyon Prizetaker   *Winter Crop*   *Musselburgh*

LETTUCE

In the average garden the cultivation of lettuce is a simple matter. A row or two is sown in spring and again in early summer — the seedlings are thinned when they are obviously over-crowded and they are cut when the heads are mature. Unfortunately such a casual approach often leads to disappointment. Pests and diseases take their toll and the survivors all mature at the same time. Buy a packet of mixed seed containing varieties which mature at different times or preferably sow in short rows at fort-nightly intervals. Another cause of dis-appointment is bolting (running to seed) before maturity — the usual reason is transplanting at the wrong time or in the wrong way. So lettuces are not quite as easy as some books suggest but with care, the right varieties and some cloches you can enjoy them nearly all year round.

Expected germination time	6 - 12 days
Approximate number of seeds per 10 gm	7000
Expected yield from a 3 m row	10 - 20 heads
Life expectancy of stored seed	3 years
Approximate time between sowing and cutting	8 - 14 weeks (cabbage and cos vars.)
Approximate time between sowing and cutting	6 - 8 weeks (loose-leaf vars.)
Ease of cultivation	Not difficult

TYPES

COS   **CABBAGE: BUTTERHEAD**   **CABBAGE: CRISPHEAD**   **LOOSE-LEAF**

CALENDAR

For a Summer/Autumn Crop

Sow outdoors in late March - late July for cutting in June - October. For a mid May - mid June crop sow under glass in early February and plant out in early March under cloches.

Month	JAN	FEB	MAR	APR	MAY	JUN	JUL	AUG	SEP	OCT	NOV	DEC
Sowing Time		▣	⌇	▓	▓	▓	▒					
Cutting Time					▒	▓	▓	▓	▓	▓		

For an Early Winter Crop

Sow a mildew-resistant variety such as Avondefiance outdoors in early August. Cover with cloches in late September — close ends with glass. Harvest period November - December.

Month	JAN	FEB	MAR	APR	MAY	JUN	JUL	AUG	SEP	OCT	NOV	DEC
Sowing Time								▓				
Cutting Time										▒	▓	▓

For a Midwinter Crop

Grow a forcing variety such as Kwiek. Sow seed under heated glass in September or October — plant out as soon as the seedlings are large enough to handle. Harvest period January - early March.

Month	JAN	FEB	MAR	APR	MAY	JUN	JUL	AUG	SEP	OCT	NOV	DEC
Sowing Time									▣ ▣ ▣	⌘ ⌘ ⌘		
Cutting Time	▓	▓	▓									

For a Spring Crop

In mild areas sow a winter-hardy variety such as Winter Density in late August - early September. Thin to 8 cm. Complete thinning to 30 cm spacing in early spring — cutting period May. For other areas sow a winter-hardy or forcing variety in mid October under cloches. Harvest period April.

Month	JAN	FEB	MAR	APR	MAY	JUN	JUL	AUG	SEP	OCT	NOV	DEC
Sowing Time								▓		⌇		
Cutting Time				▓	▓							

SOWING THE CROP

Lettuce needs non-acid soil containing adequate organic matter — it must be kept moist throughout the life of the crop. For summer lettuce choose a sunny or lightly shaded site. Dig the soil and incorporate compost in autumn or early winter. Rake the soil to produce a fine tilth shortly before sowing time and apply a general-purpose fertilizer.

Spring lettuce can only be sown without glass protection in a sunny spot in a mild area.

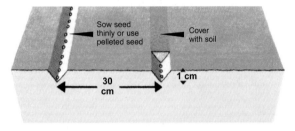

To grow lettuce for transplanting, sow 2 seeds in a small peat pot. Remove the weaker seedling after germination — harden off before transplanting.

LOOKING AFTER THE CROP

Thin the seedlings as soon as the first true leaves appear — it is essential to avoid overcrowding. Water the day before thinning. Continue thinning at intervals until the plants are 30 cm apart (Tom Thumb, Little Gem — 20 cm, Salad Bowl — 15 cm).

Lettuce hates to be moved — sow seed whenever you can where the crop is to grow. You can try transplanting seedlings — do not bury the lower leaves.

Protect against slugs and birds. Hoe regularly. Keep the plants watered — avoid watering in the evening as this will increase the chance of disease. Soil under glass should be kept on the dry side — make sure there is adequate ventilation.

Greenfly and grey mould can be serious problems — see The Pocket Garden Troubles Expert.

HARVESTING THE CROP

Lettuce is ready for cutting as soon as a firm heart has formed. Test by pressing the top of the plant gently with the back of the hand — squeezing the heart will damage the tissues.

If left at this stage the heart will begin to grow upwards — a sign that it is getting ready to bolt. You must then cut immediately for kitchen use or throw it away.

Cut in the morning when the heads have dew on them. Pull up the plant and cut off the roots and lower leaves. Put the unwanted material on the compost heap.

VARIETIES

BUTTERHEAD varieties

The most popular group. They will generally tolerate poorer conditions than other types and mature quickly. Leaves are soft and smooth edged. Most are summer varieties.

ALL THE YEAR ROUND The most popular variety — suitable for spring, summer and autumn sowing. Medium-sized.

AVONDEFIANCE A dark green and mildew-resistant variety for sowing between June and August.

BUTTERCRUNCH Dark green heads with a heart of crisp creamy leaves. Slow to bolt in dry weather.

CLARION A good choice for early sowing under glass. Virus tolerant — good mildew resistance.

DYNAMITE The first lettuce with greenfly as well as mildew resistance. Neat and compact heads.

KWIEK A forcing variety for growing under glass for an early winter crop. Large heads.

SANGRIA Something different — a red butterhead with pale green inner leaves. Some virus and mildew resistance.

TOM THUMB The favourite variety for small plots — the heads are tennis-ball size. Grow it as a summer crop.

COS varieties

Cos (romaine) lettuces have oblong heads and an upright growth habit. The leaves are crisp and the flavour is good, but they are generally more difficult to grow than other types.

LITTLE GEM A quick-maturing variety — sow early for a June crop. Small, compact heads — tie loosely with wool.

LOBJOIT'S GREEN One of the old favourites — large and self-folding. The leaves are crisp and dark green.

SHERWOOD A modern variety with crisp leaves and an outstanding flavour. Good mildew resistance.

WINTER DENSITY Compact heads with crisp, dark green hearts. Sow in August - September for an April crop.

All The Year Round

Winter Density

CRISPHEAD varieties

The popularity of the crispheads continues to increase following the success of Iceberg at the supermarkets. The large solid hearts have few outer leaves — they are less likely to bolt than the butterheads.

CHALLENGE An improvement on Saladin for sowing in the open and under cloches. Good mildew and bolting resistance.

GREAT LAKES A large dark green variety — the original summer crisphead which came from the U.S.

ICEBERG The best known crisphead, but not the best choice for growing in the garden. Sow in spring or early summer.

KELLYS A good choice for growing under glass. Sow in November - January for an April crop.

LAKELAND An Iceberg type of large crisphead which has been bred to be more reliable in British weather.

MINIGREEN Tight orange-sized heads of crunchy leaves. The hearts are creamy yellow.

SALADIN An Iceberg type with large heads of crisp leaves. Sow in April - July for a summer and autumn crop.

WEBB'S WONDERFUL You will find this large-hearted frilly lettuce in most of the catalogues. Succeeds in hot summers.

LOOSE-LEAF varieties

These types do not produce a heart. The leaves are curled and are picked like spinach — a few at a time without cutting the whole plant. Sow seeds in April or May.

FRISBY A cos/loose-leaf hybrid which matures quickly. The leaves are crisp and frilly — good mildew resistance.

LOLLO BIONDA A pale green version of the popular Lollo Rossa. Stands up well in hot conditions.

LOLLO ROSSA The curled edges of the leaves are tinged with red — adds colour as well as flavour to a salad.

SALAD BOWL The basic variety. Pick regularly and the plant will stay productive for many weeks. Red Salad Bowl is available.

Iceberg

Salad Bowl

MARROW & COURGETTE

Marrows, courgettes, squashes and pumpkins all belong to the cucumber family — fleshy-fruited vegetables which can be grown outdoors. Unfortunately there are no exact definitions and the dividing lines between them are blurred. Until recently the vegetable marrow — large, oblong and striped, was the most popular type. The usual routine is to pick it at the overgrown stage and then stuff and boil it to serve as an insipid-tasting casing for minced beef etc. Courgettes have begun to take over, and they are nothing more than selected varieties of marrows which are cut at the immature stage.

Expected germination time	5 - 8 days
Expected yield per plant	4 (marrows)
Expected yield per plant	16 (courgettes)
Approximate time between sowing and cutting	10 - 14 weeks
Ease of cultivation	Not difficult

CALENDAR

Seed should be sown in late May or early June. In the colder areas of the country it is helpful to cover the seedlings with cloches for a few weeks. The first courgettes will be ready for cutting in late July or August.

For an earlier crop the seed is sown under glass in late April. Harden off the seedlings and plant them out in early June when the danger of frost has passed.

Month	JAN	FEB	MAR	APR	MAY	JUN	JUL	AUG	SEP	OCT	NOV	DEC
Sowing Time (outdoors)						■						
Sowing Time (indoors)				■	■							
Cutting Time							■	■	■	■		

SOWING & PLANTING THE CROP

A sunny site protected from strong winds is essential. The soil must be well drained and rich in organic matter. In most cases only a few plants are required, so prepare planting pockets as shown below rather than sowing in rows.

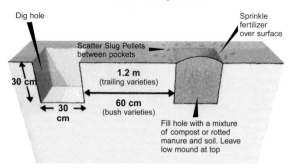

Soak the seeds overnight — sow 3 seeds 3 cm deep and about 6 cm apart at the centre of each pocket. Cover with a large jar or cloche to speed up germination. When the first true leaves have appeared thin out to leave the strongest seedlings.

Seedlings can be raised indoors but the results are usually less satisfactory. Sow a single seed edgeways 1 cm deep in compost — keep at a minimum of 18°C until germinated. Harden off before planting in pockets outdoors.

LOOKING AFTER THE CROP

Pinch out the tips of trailing varieties when the shoots are 60 cm long. Renew Slug Pellets if damage is seen. Keep the soil moist — water around the plants, not over them. Syringe lightly in dry weather. Mulch around the plants in summer before the fruits have formed.

If the weather is cold or it is early in the season, fertilize female flowers (tiny marrow behind petals) with a male flower (thin stalk behind petals). Remove a mature male flower on a dry day, fold back petals and push gently into a female flower.

Feed every 14 days with a tomato fertilizer once the fruits start to swell. Limit pumpkins to 2 per plant. Keep marrows on a tile to prevent rotting and slug attack.

HARVESTING THE CROP

Cut when the fruits are still quite small — courgettes 10 cm, marrows 20 - 25 cm. Push your thumbnail into the surface near the stalk — if it goes in quite easily then the marrow is ready for picking. Continual cropping is essential to prolong the fruiting period. Allow pumpkins, winter squashes and marrows for winter storage to mature on the plant — remove before the frosts arrive.

VARIETIES

MARROW varieties

These include all the traditional vegetable marrows grown for immediate use in summer and storage for winter.

GREEN BUSH The favourite all-rounder — cut the small fruits as courgettes and let a few mature to become marrows.

LONG GREEN TRAILING Large and cylindrical with pale stripes. Popular for kitchen use and exhibition.

TIGER CROSS An F_1 hybrid similar to Green Bush, but more productive and resistant to mosaic virus.

COURGETTE varieties

Compact bush marrows which are grown for their immature fruits which will appear over a long period if regularly removed.

DEFENDER This F_1 hybrid produces an abundant crop of green courgettes — good resistance to mosaic virus.

GOLD RUSH A yellow F_1 hybrid which has replaced Golden Zucchini in the popular catalogues.

ZUCCHINI The basic green variety which appears in many catalogues — now losing ground to the F_1 hybrids.

SQUASH varieties

The summer squashes are non-standard shaped marrows — the winter squashes have a hard rind and fibrous flesh.

BUTTERNUT (winter) Club-shaped fruits with orange flesh. Does best in mild southern areas.

CUSTARD SQUASH (summer) Patty Pan in the U.S. Use these scalloped-edged flat fruits like courgettes.

VEGETABLE SPAGHETTI (winter) After boiling spaghetti-like strands are scraped out with a fork.

PUMPKIN varieties

These varieties include the large edible gourds — thick-skinned, round or oval and grown to maturity on the plant.

ATLANTIC GIANT This is the one to grow if you want to win the Largest Pumpkin competition.

Green Bush

Gold Rush

Vegetable Spaghetti

ONION from sets

Sets (small onions) have several advantages over seeds — they are quicker maturing, hardier and less prone to onion fly and mildew. In addition less skill and less soil fertility are required, but there is the extra cost to consider and also the extra risk of bolting.

Expected sprouting time	11 - 14 days
Approximate number of sets per kg	170 (onions)
Approximate number of sets per kg	70 (shallots)
Expected yield from a 3 m row	3 kg
Approximate time between planting and lifting	20 weeks
Ease of cultivation	Easy

CALENDAR

Month	JAN	FEB	MAR	APR	MAY	JUN	JUL	AUG	SEP	OCT	NOV	DEC
Planting Time		▓	▓	▓								
Lifting Time								▓	▓			

PLANTING THE CROP

All onions need good soil and free drainage, but sets require neither the fine tilth nor the high humus content which is necessary for seed-sown onions. Dig in early winter and incorporate compost if available. Lime if necessary. Firm the surface before planting and rake in a general-purpose fertilizer.

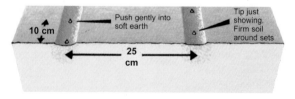

Plant onion sets 10 cm apart in mid March - mid April. Shallots require wider (15 cm) and earlier (mid February - mid March) planting.

LOOKING AFTER THE CROP

If birds are a nuisance in your area protect the sets with black thread or netting. Keep weed-free by hoeing and hand pulling. Push back any sets which have been lifted by frost or birds. Treat as for seed-sown onions (see page 79) once the sets are established and shoots have appeared.

HARVESTING THE CROP

Shallots: The leaves will turn yellow in July. Lift the clusters and separate them, allowing each shallot to dry thoroughly. Remove dirt and brittle stems, and store in net bags in a cool dry place for up to 8 months.
   Onions: See page 79.

VARIETIES

AILSA CRAIG (onion) An old favourite — round, large and straw-coloured with mild-flavoured flesh.

GOLDEN GOURMET (shallot) Smooth golden bulbs which have taken over from Dutch Yellow. Stores well.

JET SET (onion) Round golden onions which mature about 2 weeks before most other varieties.

RED BARON (onion) This red-skinned variety is available as heat-treated sets — the risk of bolting is removed.

RED SUN (shallot) Shiny red-tinged bulbs which have taken over from Dutch Red. Good resistance to bolting.

SETTON (onion) A modern variety bred from Sturon — it is claimed to be higher yielding with a longer storage life.

STUTTGARTER GIANT (onion) The flattened bulbs have a good flavour — until recently the most popular variety.

Ailsa Craig

Red Sun

ONION from seed

It is surprising that onions are much less popular as a home-grown vegetable than peas and beans. Few vegetables have so many uses in the kitchen and therefore they are in constant demand. The new Japanese varieties have filled the June - July gap of the old days, and from a couple of carefully-timed sowings we can have onions fresh from the garden or out of store almost all year round. Salad onions can be kept in the refrigerator for up to a week. Do not store bulbs in this way — keep in a cool place until required.

Expected germination time	21 days
Approximate number of seeds per 10 gm	3000
Expected yield from a 3 m row	4 kg
Approximate time between sowing and lifting	46 weeks (August-sown vars.)
Approximate time between sowing and lifting	22 weeks (spring-sown vars.)
Ease of cultivation	Easy

CALENDAR

For an August or September crop sow as soon as the land is workable in spring (late February - early April).

For an earlier crop sow in mid August. Japanese varieties mature in late June — standard varieties such as Ailsa Craig are later cropping and less reliable but they can be stored.

In cold areas and for exhibition sow under glass in January, harden off in March and transplant outdoors in April.

Sow salad onions in March - July for a June - October crop. Sow in August for onions in March - May.

Month	JAN	FEB	MAR	APR	MAY	JUN	JUL	AUG	SEP	OCT	NOV	DEC
Sowing Time (outdoors)			█					█				
Sowing Time (indoors)	█			🌱								
Lifting Time							█	█	█			

78

SOWING & PLANTING THE CROP

Choose an open sunny site with good drainage. Dig thoroughly in autumn, incorporating well-rotted manure or compost. Lime in late winter if necessary. Before sowing or planting apply a general-purpose fertilizer and rake the surface when the soil is reasonably dry. Tread over the area and then rake again to produce a fine, even tilth.

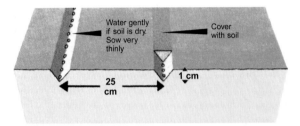

Water gently if soil is dry. Sow very thinly

Cover with soil

25 cm

1 cm

Thin the spring-sown crop in 2 stages when the soil is moist — first to 3 - 5 cm when the seedlings have straightened up and then to 10 cm apart. Seeds of Japanese varieties should be sown at 3 cm intervals in rows 20 cm apart. Thin seedlings to 10 cm intervals in spring.

Seedlings raised under glass should be transplanted 10 cm apart, leaving 20 cm between the rows. Let the roots fall vertically in the planting hole — the bulb base should be about 1 cm below the surface. Plant firmly.

Salad onions should be planted in rows 10 cm apart. Thin, if necessary, to 3 cm spacings.

LOOKING AFTER THE CROP

Hoe carefully or weed by hand. Water if the soil is dry and feed occasionally. Break off any flower stems which appear. Mulching will reduce the need for watering and weeding. Stop watering once the onions have swollen and pull back the covering mulch or earth to expose the bulbs to the sun.

HARVESTING THE CROP

Salad varieties should be pulled when the bulbs are 1 - 3 cm across. The harvesting season is March - October.

Bulb varieties are mature when the foliage is yellow and topples over. Leave for 2 weeks and then lift with a fork on a dry day. Onions not for immediate use should be dried. Spread out on sacking or in trays — move indoors if the weather is rainy.

Drying takes 7 - 21 days, depending on bulb size and the air temperature — do not store bulbs which are soft, spotted or have abnormally thick necks. Store the onions in trays or nets in a cool and well-lit place — they should keep until late spring. Do not store Japanese varieties.

VARIETIES

BULB varieties

Standard varieties are grown for their large bulbs which can be stored during the winter months. Most of them are only suitable for spring sowing but a few can be sown in August for a late July crop. August sowing of Japanese varieties is more reliable.

AILSA CRAIG The variety you will find in all the catalogues — very large but not a good keeper.

BEDFORDSHIRE CHAMPION Stores better than Ailsa Craig but it is very susceptible to downy mildew.

HYGRO An F$_1$ hybrid which is widely available — heavy, globe-shaped and suitable for storage.

KELSAE A good choice if you want to grow giant onions for the show bench. Globular, red-tinted skin.

RED BARON The most popular red-skinned onion. An early variety with flattish bulbs which store well.

RELIANCE A standard variety which can be sown in August for a midsummer crop next season.

SENSHYU The only Japanese variety you are likely to find in the popular catalogues. Grow it for June - July onions.

SALAD varieties

Other names: Spring or bunching onions. White-skinned and mild-flavoured varieties grown specifically for salad use.

ISHIKURA The long white stems do not form bulbs. Pull as required — most of the plant can be eaten.

WHITE LISBON By far the most popular variety. Can provide salad onions for 6 months of the year.

PICKLING varieties

Varieties grown for their 'button' bulbs which are sown in April and lifted in July - August for pickling.

PARIS SILVER SKIN The favourite pickling onion. Do not thin the seedlings — lift when the bulb is the size of a marble.

Ailsa Craig *White Lisbon* *Paris Silver Skin*

PARSNIP

Parsnips need very little attention and radish or lettuce can be grown between the rows. The roots can be left in the ground in winter to be dug up as required, but they are not popular as they are too strongly flavoured for most people. A short-growing variety is usually the best choice.

Expected germination time	10 - 28 days
Approximate number of seeds per 10 gm	3000
Expected yield from a 3 m row	4 kg
Approximate time between sowing and lifting	34 weeks
Ease of cultivation	Easy

CALENDAR

Month	JAN	FEB	MAR	APR	MAY	JUN	JUL	AUG	SEP	OCT	NOV	DEC
Sowing Time												
Lifting Time												

SOWING THE CROP

Long parsnips need a deep and friable soil but any soil in sun or light shade can grow a good crop of a shorter variety. Dig in autumn or early winter — do not add compost or fresh manure but lime if necessary. Rake in a general-purpose fertilizer when preparing the seed bed.

Sow in March — with a short-rooted variety you can sow in April.

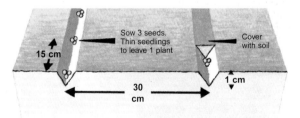

15 cm

Sow 3 seeds.
Thin seedlings
to leave 1 plant

Cover
with soil

30 cm

1 cm

LOOKING AFTER THE CROP

Hoe regularly to keep down weeds — do not touch the crowns of the plants. The crop requires very little attention and is not usually attacked by pests, but it will be necessary to water when there is a prolonged dry spell.

HARVESTING THE CROP

The roots are ready for lifting when the leaves begin to die down in autumn. Lift the crop as required, using a fork to loosen the soil. Leave the remainder in the soil for harvesting later. It is a good idea to lift some in November and to store them in the same way as carrots (see page 40). In this way you will have a supply of parsnips when the soil is frozen. Lift and store any remaining roots at the end of February.

VARIETIES

ARROW One of a series of narrow-shouldered parsnips (Javelin, Lancer, etc) which can be grown as baby vegetables.

AVONRESISTER One of the shortest — 12 cm long roots with canker resistance. Sow at 8 cm intervals.

GLADIATOR The first F_1 hybrid parsnip. Tapered root with smooth skin — high resistance to canker.

HOLLOW CROWN IMPROVED Long tapered roots for kitchen and exhibition. Good flavour.

TENDER & TRUE Long-rooted variety for kitchen and exhibition. Very little core — high resistance to canker.

THE STUDENT An old long-rooted variety with creamy white flesh and an outstanding flavour.

WHITE GEM Broad-shouldered tapered roots — high canker resistance. Medium-sized — easy to lift.

Avonresister

Tender & True

PEA

Quite often peas are disappointing as a garden crop. The yield can be quite small for the area occupied, and if the soil is poor or the weather is hot it can seem that the amount obtained is not worth all the trouble. But if you want to discover how good peas can taste then pick the pods when they are quite small and within an hour boil the shelled peas for about 10 minutes in a small amount of water.

There are many types of peas and their classification is complex. There are garden peas and also mangetout, which are sown in April or May and cooked whole. There are round and wrinkled peas, tall and dwarf plants, and first early, second early and maincrop varieties. Never sow peas in cold and wet soil, make sure that the soil is fertile, keep the birds away and spray when necessary.

Expected germination time	7 - 10 days
Approximate number of seeds per 100 ml	200
Amount required for a 3 m row	50 ml
Expected yield from a 3 m row	5 kg
Approximate time between autumn sowing and picking	32 weeks
Approximate time between autumn sowing and picking	12 - 16 weeks
Ease of cultivation	Not easy

TYPES

ROUND PEA (dried)   **WRINKLED PEA** (dried)   **MANGETOUT**   **PETIT POIS**

CALENDAR

For a May/June Crop
Pick a sheltered site — expect some losses if the site is cold and wet. Grow a round variety — Feltham First is widely available and reliable for both early spring and late sowings. Cover seedlings and plants with cloches.

Month	JAN	FEB	MAR	APR	MAY	JUN	JUL	AUG	SEP	OCT	NOV	DEC
Sowing Time		▨	▨							▨	▨	
Picking Time						▮						

For a June/July Crop
For sowing in mid March choose a round variety or a first early wrinkled variety such as Kelvedon Wonder or Early Onward. For sowing in late March or April pick a second early wrinkled type — Onward is a popular choice.

Month	JAN	FEB	MAR	APR	MAY	JUN	JUL	AUG	SEP	OCT	NOV	DEC
Sowing Time			▮									
Picking Time							▮					

For an August Crop
Sow a maincrop wrinkled variety in April or May. Height is one of the most important points to consider — tall-growing ones like Alderman need nearly 2 m between the rows. If space is limited choose Senator.

Month	JAN	FEB	MAR	APR	MAY	JUN	JUL	AUG	SEP	OCT	NOV	DEC
Sowing Time				▮	▮							
Picking Time								▮	▮			

For a September/October Crop
Sow in June or July for a September - October crop. It is necessary to choose the right variety — a first early wrinkled variety with good mildew resistance. Pioneer is a suitable choice but it is hard to find.

Month	JAN	FEB	MAR	APR	MAY	JUN	JUL	AUG	SEP	OCT	NOV	DEC
Sowing Time						▮	▮					
Picking Time									▮	▮		

SOWING THE CROP

Peas need non-acid soil which has a good crumbly structure and adequate humus. Choose an open site which has not grown peas for at least 2 seasons. Dig the soil in autumn or early winter, incorporating 2 bucketsful of compost or well-rotted manure in each square metre of soil. Apply a light dressing of a general-purpose fertilizer shortly before sowing time — do not over-feed.

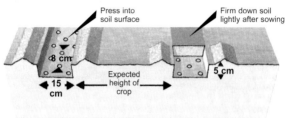

Press into soil surface

Firm down soil lightly after sowing

8 cm

15 cm

Expected height of crop

5 cm

LOOKING AFTER THE CROP

You must protect the rows from birds immediately after sowing. Do not rely on a chemical deterrent — place twiggy branches over the surface or use plastic netting. Wire-mesh guards are best of all.

Hoe regularly to keep weeds under control. When the seedlings are about 8 cm high insert twigs alongside the stems to provide support. Do not delay this operation — leaving the stems to straggle over the ground will encourage slugs. Medium- and tall-growing varieties will need additional support — erect a sturdy screen of plastic netting along each row.

Water during dry weather in summer. Mulch between the rows in order to conserve moisture. Maggoty peas are a familiar problem. The best way to avoid trouble is to sow a quick-maturing crop early or late in the season.

HARVESTING THE CROP

A pod is ready for picking when it is well filled but while there is still a little air space between each pea. Start harvesting at this stage, beginning at the bottom of the stem and working upwards. Use both hands, one to hold the stem and the other to pick off the pod.

Pick regularly — pods left to mature on the plant will seriously reduce further pod production. If you harvest too many for immediate use then keep the excess in the refrigerator or deep freeze them.

Use the stems for making compost when all the pods have been picked. Leave the roots in the soil.

Allow the pods to mature on the stems if you intend to dry the peas. In wet weather lift the plants and hang indoors in bundles until the pods are ripe.

VARIETIES

ROUND varieties

The peas remain smooth and round when dried. They are all first earlies — hardier, quicker maturing and more able to stand poor conditions than the wrinkled ones.

DOUCE PROVENCE 45 cm. This variety is not grown for maximum yields — maximum sweetness is its claim to fame.

FELTHAM FIRST 45 cm. A popular choice for early spring and late autumn sowing. Needs little support.

FORTUNE 45 cm. Quite similar to Feltham First — matures rather later but yields are higher.

METEOR 30 cm. This dwarf is one of the hardiest of all pea varieties. Small, well-filled pods.

WRINKLED varieties

The peas are wrinkled when dried. The plants are larger and heavier cropping than the round ones.

ALDERMAN (maincrop) 1.5 m. Popular with exhibitors — the pods contain 11 large peas. Prolonged cropping season.

CAVALIER (second early) 75 cm. A vigorous variety with long, pointed pods. High yielding with resistance to mildew.

EARLY ONWARD (first early) 60 cm. Not as popular as Onward but it does mature about 10 days earlier.

HURST GREEN SHAFT (second early) 75 cm. A popular choice for exhibition and kitchen use. Resistant to mildew.

KELVEDON WONDER (first early) 45 cm. A popular variety for successional sowing from March to July.

LITTLE MARVEL (first early) 45 cm. The blunt-ended pods are borne in pairs. Good flavour.

ONWARD (second early) 75 cm. The favourite garden pea. Pods are plump, blunt-ended and dark green.

SENATOR (maincrop) 75 cm. Pods borne in pairs. A good maincrop for a small garden but not in many catalogues.

Feltham First

Kelvedon Wonder

MANGETOUT varieties

Pick before the peas swell and cook the pods whole. Begin sowing when the soil has started to warm up in April.

Month	JAN	FEB	MAR	APR	MAY	JUN	JUL	AUG	SEP	OCT	NOV	DEC
Sowing Time												
Picking Time												

DELIKATA 75 cm. A wrinkled dual-purpose variety — use as a mangetout when young or shell as a garden pea when mature.

OREGON SUGAR POD 1 m. Popular variety with 2 cm wide pods — pick when 8 cm long. Good disease resistance.

SUGAR DWARF SWEET GREEN 1 m. Very similar to the much more popular Oregon Sugar Pod.

SUGAR GEM 60 cm. Yields are high and the pods are stringless, but it needs good growing conditions.

SUGAR SNAP 1.5 m. Cook young pods whole or leave to mature and shell like garden peas. Thick, juicy pods.

PETIT POIS varieties

Dwarf varieties which produce unusually sweet tiny peas. Begin sowing when the soil has started to warm up in April.

Month	JAN	FEB	MAR	APR	MAY	JUN	JUL	AUG	SEP	OCT	NOV	DEC
Sowing Time												
Picking Time												

WAVEREX 60 cm. The only petit pois variety you are likely to find. Eat raw in salads or cook with salad onions.

Oregon Sugar Pod

Waverex

POTATO

If you have a large plot then you can grow both early and maincrop varieties — earlies to give you 'new' potatoes in summer and maincrops to provide tubers for storage over winter. If space is limited then an early variety should be your only choice. Yields will be lower than from a maincrop but it will take up less space, miss the damaging effect of blight and will provide new potatoes when shop prices are high. Buy good quality seed and chit them before planting — this technique induces the production of small shoots (see page 89). Greening of developing tubers must be prevented by earthing-up — the covering of the stem bases with soil.

Amount required for a 3 m row	750 gm
Expected yield from a 3 m row	5 kg (early vars.)
Expected yield from a 3 m row	9 kg (maincrop vars.)
Approximate time between planting and lifting	13 weeks (early vars.)
Approximate time between planting and lifting	22 weeks (maincrop vars.)
Ease of cultivation	Not difficult

CALENDAR

First early varieties: Plant seed potatoes in late March — in southern areas you can plant in mid March but delay until early April in the north. Lift in June or July.

Second early varieties: Plant in early to mid April — lift in July or August.

Maincrop varieties: Plant in mid to late April. Tubers can be lifted in August for immediate use but potatoes for storage should be lifted in September or early October.

Month	JAN	FEB	MAR	APR	MAY	JUN	JUL	AUG	SEP	OCT	NOV	DEC
Planting Time			▓	▓								
Lifting Time						▓	▓		▓			

PLANTING THE CROP

Potatoes can be grown in practically every soil type, but do not grow on land which has been used for this crop within the past 2 seasons. Choose a sunny spot and avoid frost pockets. Dig the soil in autumn and add compost if the soil was not manured for the previous crop. Before planting break down any clods and sprinkle a general-purpose fertilizer over the surface.

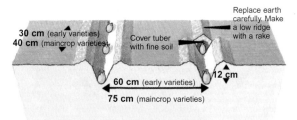

30 cm (early varieties)
40 cm (maincrop varieties)

Cover tuber with fine soil

Replace earth carefully. Make a low ridge with a rake

60 cm (early varieties)
75 cm (maincrop varieties)

12 cm

Chit the seed potatoes when you obtain them in February — this is vital for earlies and advisable for maincrops. Set them out rose end (where most of the eyes are) uppermost in egg boxes or wooden trays. Keep them in a light (not sunny) frost-free place — in about 6 weeks there will be several 1 - 3 cm long sturdy shoots.

LOOKING AFTER THE CROP

Draw a little soil over emerging shoots if there is danger of frosts. Earth-up when the stems are about 25 cm high — do this by breaking up the soil between the rows with a fork and then piling the loose soil with a draw hoe against the stems. Aim to produce a flat-topped ridge about 15 cm high.

Water liberally in dry weather — this is most important once the tubers have started to form.

HARVESTING THE CROP

With earlies wait until the flowers open or the buds drop. Carefully remove soil from a small part of the ridge and examine the tubers. They are ready for lifting as new potatoes when they are the size of hens' eggs — push a flat-tined fork into the ridge well away from the stems and lift the roots forward into the trench between the ridges.

With maincrops for storage cut off the stems once the foliage has turned brown and the stalks have withered. Remove the cut stems and wait for 10 days before lifting the roots — this is to ensure that all blight spores on the leaves have died. Pick off the tubers and let them dry for several hours. Place them in a wooden box and store in a dark, frost-free shed — they should keep until spring.

After harvesting remove all tubers from the soil, however small, to avoid problems next year.

VARIETIES

FIRST EARLY varieties

ARRAN PILOT Long, white flesh. An old favourite now being replaced by modern varieties. Does best in sandy soil.

DUKE OF YORK Oval, yellow flesh. Succeeds in all areas and soil types — renowned for its flavour.

EPICURE Round, white flesh. An old variety which is hardier than most on cold, exposed sites.

MARIS BARD Oval, white flesh. Very early — produces heavy crops of waxy, well-flavoured tubers.

PREMIERE Round, pale cream flesh. Very early — waxy rather than floury. Good disease tolerance.

SHARPE'S EXPRESS Long, white flesh. Still in the catalogues because of its keeping and cooking qualities.

SWIFT Round, white flesh. Very early — good resistance to virus and eelworm. Low-growing.

VANESSA Long, yellow flesh. The red-skinned first early — matures rather late but better than most in dry weather.

SECOND EARLY varieties

CATRIONA Long, pale yellow flesh. Distinctive blue eyes. Good flavour, but does not store well.

CHARLOTTE Long, pale yellow flesh. Waxy and firm when cooked — an excellent salad potato.

ESTIMA Oval, pale yellow flesh. A reliable waxy variety which provides attractively-shaped tubers and heavy yields.

KESTREL Long, cream flesh. Violet eyes. Unusually high resistance to slug damage.

NADINE Round, white flesh. A modern popular early for show bench and kitchen. Smooth skin, good eelworm resistance.

WILJA Oval, pale yellow flesh. High yielding with good cooking qualities. Recommended as a salad potato.

Duke of York

Wilja

MAINCROP varieties

ARRAN VICTORY Oval, white flesh. A purple-skinned variety — floury texture, good flavour.

CARA Round, cream flesh. Pink-blotched like King Edward, but more blight- and drought-resistant. Heavy cropper.

DESIREE Oval, pale yellow flesh. This pink-skinned variety is hard to beat.

GOLDEN WONDER Long, yellow flesh. One of the best for flavour, but yields are not high. Needs good soil.

KERR'S PINK Round, white flesh. An early maincrop for gardeners in wet and heavy soil areas.

KING EDWARD Oval, cream flesh. An old favourite — grow it if you want quality rather than quantity.

MAJESTIC Long, white flesh. No longer in all the catalogues but still a fine potato for making chips.

MARIS PIPER Oval, cream flesh. Excellent yields, but slug and drought resistance are low.

PENTLAND CROWN Oval, white flesh. A late variety which outyields the others, but cooking qualities are moderate.

PINK FIR APPLE Long, yellow flesh. A waxy maincrop with a new potato taste. Late maturing, modest yields.

REMARKA Oval, yellow flesh. Waxy texture, good resistance to blight and eelworm. Heavy cropper.

ROMANO Oval, white flesh. A red-skinned variety — waxy-textured tubers with good cooking and keeping qualities.

CHRISTMAS POTATOES

Growing potatoes for Christmas dinner is a gamble, but it is worth trying as very little effort is required. When lifting your crop of first earlies in July put a few tubers aside. Plant them without delay in a warm spot in the garden and look after them in the normal way. In late September cover the plants with large cloches and fork up the tubers (hopefully) on Christmas Eve.

Desiree

Pentland Crown

RADISH

Summer radishes are practically trouble-free and the round or thumb-long red roots are ready for salads or sandwiches about a month after sowing — the popular varieties are often grown as space fillers between rows of peas or carrots. It is a pity that so many gardeners stop there, when there are unusual varieties to try — small pink roots, giant Japanese varieties etc. In addition there are the large winter radishes which can reach 30 cm or more. They are easily grown for winter use in salads or as a cooked vegetable.

Expected germination time	4 - 7 days
Approximate number of seeds per 10 gm	1000
Expected yield from a 3 m row	2 kg (summer vars.)
Expected yield from a 3 m row	5 kg (winter vars.)
Life expectancy of stored seed	6 years
Approximate time between sowing and lifting	3 - 6 weeks (summer vars.)
Approximate time between sowing and lifting	10 - 12 weeks (winter vars.)
Ease of cultivation	Easy

CALENDAR

Summer varieties: Sow under cloches in January or February — sow outdoors in March. For a prolonged supply sow every few weeks or use 'Mixed Radish' seed which consists of varieties which mature at different rates. Sowing after early June can be unreliable.

Winter varieties: Sow in July or early August. Begin lifting roots in late October.

Month	JAN	FEB	MAR	APR	MAY	JUN	JUL	AUG	SEP	OCT	NOV	DEC
Sowing Time												
Lifting Time												

SOWING THE CROP

The soil requirement for radishes is usually given very little thought — any odd patch will do. But for maximum tenderness and flavour the crop must be grown quickly and this calls for some soil preparation.

Choose a sunny spot for early sowing but later crops need some shade. Dig compost into the soil if it was not manured for a previous crop — apply a general-purpose fertilizer before sowing and rake the surface to a fine tilth.

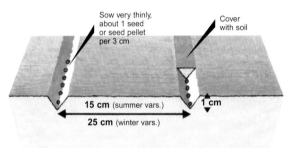

Sow very thinly, about 1 seed or seed pellet per 3 cm

Cover with soil

15 cm (summer vars.)

25 cm (winter vars.)

1 cm

LOOKING AFTER THE CROP

With the summer varieties little or no thinning should be necessary — if there is any overcrowding then thin immediately so that the plants are spaced at 3 cm (small varieties) or 5 - 10 cm (larger and Japanese varieties). With winter radishes thin to leave the plants 15 cm apart — make sure you carry out this thinning before the plants are overcrowded.

Protect the plants against birds if they are a nuisance in your garden. Spray with an insecticide if flea beetles begin to perforate the leaves.

Quick and uninterrupted growth is essential for good results, so hoe to keep down weeds and water when the weather is dry. Summer radish sown in July and August is often disappointing because of hot and dry weather — swelling can be poor and the roots may be woody and peppery.

HARVESTING THE CROP

Pull the summer varieties when the globular ones are about 2.5 cm across and the intermediates are no longer than your thumb. They can grow much longer but these overgrown specimens are woody and hollow.

Japanese varieties are not pulled until they are 15 cm long — they can be allowed to grow longer if required for cooking rather than salads.

The winter varieties can be left in the ground and lifted as required, provided you cover the crowns with straw or peat. It is usually a better plan, however, to lift them in November and then store them in the same way as carrots (see page 40).

VARIETIES

SUMMER varieties

By far the more popular group. Globular ones are ball-shaped, the intermediate varieties are cylindrical and are pulled when 6 - 8 cm and the long varieties which may grow up to 30 cm.

APRIL CROSS Long, white. A mooli or Japanese radish. Sow in April onwards — lift when 15 - 30 cm long.

CHERRY BELLE Globular, all-red. Very popular. Mild flavour. Slow to go woody.

FLAMBOYANT SABINA Intermediate, red/white. A good choice if you are looking for a radish with a strong flavour.

FRENCH BREAKFAST Intermediate, red/white. Very popular. Quick-growing — mild when picked at the right time.

LONG WHITE ICICLE Long, white. Crisp and nutty-flavoured, but not popular. Lift when 8 - 15 cm long.

PINK BEAUTY Globular, pink. A change from the usual white and red for the salad bowl.

PRINZ ROTIN Globular, all-red. Unlike older varieties it is reputed to keep its crispness and mildness when oversized.

SCARLET GLOBE Globular, all-red. Popular. A good choice for poor soils and early sowing.

SPARKLER 3 Globular, red/white. The round red radish with a white patch at the root end. Very quick maturing.

WINTER varieties

The roots are large, weighing up to a kilo or more. They have white, black or pink skins and a stronger flavour than the summer varieties.

BLACK SPANISH ROUND Black. Large globular roots with white flesh — very hot when eaten raw.

CHINA ROSE Dark pink. The baby of the group with roots which are 15 cm long and 5 cm wide.

MANTANGHONG Green/white. This tennis ball-sized radish has red flesh and a unique nutty flavour.

Scarlet Globe

French Breakfast

China Rose

SPINACH

Grow this vegetable only if the family likes it, and that calls for learning to cook it properly. Pick young leaves and steam them quickly using the water on the washed leaves — add no extra water. There are two types of true spinach — they are both annuals which are picked either in summer (round-seeded varieties) or during winter and spring (mostly prickly-seeded varieties). The half-hardy New Zealand spinach is not spinach at all although its leaves are used in the same way, and perpetual spinach (spinach beet) is really a type of leaf beet — see page 22. For maximum flavour and tenderness grow a summer variety.

Expected germination time	12 - 20 days
Approximate number of seeds per 10 gm	500
Expected yield from a 3 m row	2 - 5 kg
Life expectancy of stored seed	4 years
Approximate time between sowing and picking	8 - 14 weeks
Ease of cultivation	Not easy

CALENDAR

Summer varieties: Sow every few weeks from mid March to late May for picking between late May and the end of October.

Winter varieties: Sow in August and again in September for picking between October and April.

New Zealand variety: Sow in late May for picking between June and September.

Month	JAN	FEB	MAR	APR	MAY	JUN	JUL	AUG	SEP	OCT	NOV	DEC
Sowing Time			▓		▓			▓	▓			
Picking Time	▓	▓	▓	▓		▓	▓	▓	▓	▓	▓	▓

95

SOWING THE CROP

The soil must be fertile and humus-rich in order to avoid a bitter-tasting crop. The ideal place for summer spinach is between rows of tall-growing vegetables — the dappled shade will reduce the risk of the plants running to seed. Sow winter and New Zealand spinach in a sunny spot.

Dig deeply in winter and apply lime if necessary. Rake in a general-purpose fertilizer about 2 weeks before sowing.

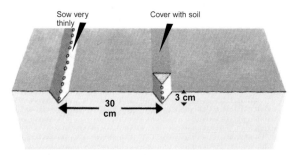

New Zealand spinach needs more space. Sow 3 seeds about 2 cm below the surface, spacing the groups 60 cm apart. Thin each group to 1 plant.

LOOKING AFTER THE CROP

Thin the seedlings of summer and winter varieties to 8 cm apart as soon as they are large enough to handle. Remove alternate plants a few weeks later for kitchen use — do not delay thinning. Hoe to keep down weeds. Water copiously during dry spells in summer.

Winter varieties will need some sort of protection from October onwards unless you live in a mild area. Use cloches or straw to cover the plants.

HARVESTING THE CROP

Start picking as soon as the leaves have reached a reasonable size. Always take the outer leaves, which should still be at the young and tender stage.

The secret of success with spinach is to pick continually so that fresh growth is encouraged. With a summer variety you can take up to half the leaves without damaging the plant — with a winter variety it is necessary to pick more sparingly. Take care when harvesting. Pick off the leaves with your fingernails — don't wrench them off as this can damage the stems or roots.

The rules for New Zealand spinach are different — pull off a few young shoots from the base of the plant at each harvesting session. A single sowing will last throughout the summer if you pick little and often.

VARIETIES

SUMMER varieties

Round-seeded varieties which provide an early and tender crop. Hot and dry weather is a problem — some varieties rapidly bolt (run to seed).

BLOOMSDALE A dark green variety which is listed in some popular catalogues. Good resistance to bolting.

KING OF DENMARK Once a favourite variety but no longer easy to find. Prone to bolt in dry weather.

MEDANIA A variety with several plus points — vigorous growth, good mildew resistance and slow to bolt.

NORVAK A typical example of the newer varieties — improved yields and reduced risk of running to seed.

SPACE An F₁ hybrid with thick, dark green leaves. Some resistance to mildew.

TRIADE An F₁ hybrid with round, dark green leaves. Reputed to be a very heavy cropper.

WINTER varieties

Prickly-seeded varieties (exception — Sigmaleaf) which provide a harvest of greens from October to April. Use only young leaves for cooking. Not easy to find in the catalogues.

BROAD-LEAVED PRICKLY A standard winter variety. Dark, fleshy foliage on plants which are slow to bolt.

DOMINANT This old favourite is no longer to be found in the popular catalogues. Good resistance to bolting.

MONNOPA A fine-flavoured variety with a low oxalic acid content — recommended as the spinach for baby food.

SIGMALEAF A round-seeded winter variety. Can also be grown as a long-lasting summer spinach.

NEW ZEALAND variety

Not a true spinach — it is a dwarf and rambling plant with soft and fleshy leaves. Sow when the danger of frost has passed. The flavour is mild — does well in hot and dry weather.

Norvak

New Zealand Spinach

SWEDE

Few crops are as straightforward to grow. All you have to do is sprinkle some seeds in late spring or early summer, thin a few weeks later and then lift the large globular roots as you need them from autumn until spring. Swedes are closely related to turnips but the plants are hardier, the yields are greater and the flavour is sweeter.

Expected germination time	6 - 10 days
Approximate number of seeds per 10 gm	3000
Expected yield from a 3 m row	13 kg
Approximate time between sowing and lifting	20 - 24 weeks
Ease of cultivation	Easy

CALENDAR

Month	JAN	FEB	MAR	APR	MAY	JUN	JUL	AUG	SEP	OCT	NOV	DEC
Sowing Time												
Lifting Time												

SOWING THE CROP

Like other members of the cabbage family this crop needs a firm, non-acid soil which drains reasonably freely.

Pick a sunny location and dig in autumn — lime if necessary. In spring apply a general-purpose fertilizer to the surface — prepare the seed bed about a week later.

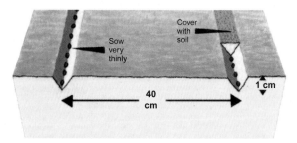

Sow very thinly

Cover with soil

40 cm

1 cm

LOOKING AFTER THE CROP

Thin out as soon as the seedlings are large enough to handle. Do this in stages until the plants are 25 cm apart.

Keep the soil hoed and water in dry weather — failure to do so will result in small and woody roots. Rain following a dry spell will cause the roots to split.

HARVESTING THE CROP

Begin lifting in early autumn when the roots are large enough to use — there is no need to wait until they have reached their maximum size. You can leave them in the soil and lift with a fork as required until spring, but it may be more convenient to lift in December and store them indoors for later use. Do this by twisting off the leaves before placing the roots between layers of sand in a stout box. Store in a cool shed.

VARIETIES

ACME Purple-topped roots which are ready for lifting from early October. Large with a good texture.

BEST OF ALL A purple-skinned yellow-fleshed variety you will find in many catalogues. Very hardy and reliable.

LIZZY Like Ruby a variety bred for extra sweetness. Good tolerance against bolting and cracking.

MARIAN Like Best of All a popular choice — high yields, good flavour and some resistance to club root and mildew.

MELFORT A green-topped variety with some resistance against cabbage root fly. Sweet taste.

RUBY Bred for extra sweetness. More resistant than most to powdery mildew.

Marian

Ruby

SWEET CORN

Once picked the sugar in the kernels is steadily converted into starch, which is why the flavour of home-grown sweet corn cooked within an hour of picking is so much better than shop-bought corn. Choose one of the early F_1 hybrids and in April raise the seedlings indoors in peat pots for planting outdoors once the danger of frost has passed. Set them out in a sheltered sunny spot and it would have to be a poor summer for this crop to fail as far north as Lancashire or Yorkshire. The 15 - 20 cm long cobs are borne on 1 - 2 m stems. The tassels at the top of the plant are the male flowers — the female flowers ('silks') are at the top of the immature cobs.

Expected germination time	10 - 12 days
Amount of seeds required for a 3 m row	2 gm
Expected yield from a 3 m row	10 cobs
Approximate time between sowing and picking	14 weeks
Ease of cultivation	Not difficult

CALENDAR

Southern counties: Sow outdoors in mid May — the cobs should be ready for picking in late August or September. For extra reliability and an earlier crop (late July onwards in mild areas) sow under glass as described below.

Other counties: Sow seeds under glass in mid April - early May and plant out in late May - early June. Alternatively sow outdoors under cloches in mid May. Place cloches in position about 2 weeks before sowing.

Month	JAN	FEB	MAR	APR	MAY	JUN	JUL	AUG	SEP	OCT	NOV	DEC
Sowing Time (Outdoors)					▨							
Sowing Time (Indoors)				▨	✿							
Picking Time								▨	▨			

SOWING & PLANTING THE CROP

Good drainage and adequate humus are necessary. Ideally the soil should be slightly acid, reasonably fertile and deep, but the situation is more important than the soil type.

Choose a sheltered spot in full sun. Dig in winter, incorporating old compost if the previous crop was not manured. Rake in a general-purpose fertilizer about 2 weeks before sowing or planting.

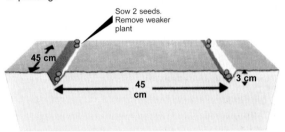

Sow 2 seeds. Remove weaker plant

45 cm

45 cm

3 cm

Sow or plant in rectangular blocks, not as a single row. This will ensure effective wind pollination of the female flowers.

Outdoor sowing may be reliable in the south but in other areas sow under cloches or preferably in pots indoors. Root disturbance must be avoided, so use peat pots rather than clay or plastic ones. Sow 2 seeds about 3 cm deep in compost — remove the weaker seedling. Harden off before planting out — set the transplants 45 cm apart.

LOOKING AFTER THE CROP

Remove cloches when the foliage touches the glass. Protect seedlings if birds are a nuisance. Remove weeds but do not hoe close to the plants.

Cover roots which appear at the base of the stem with soil or old compost. Side shoots should not be removed. Water in dry weather — this is especially important at flowering time. Stake if the plants are tall and the site is exposed.

Tap the tassels at the top of each stem in late June or July to help pollination. Apply a liquid fertilizer when the cobs begin to swell.

HARVESTING THE CROP

Each plant will produce 1 or 2 cobs. Test for ripeness when the silks (thread-like female flowers at the top of each cob) have turned chocolate brown. Pull back part of the outer sheath and squeeze a couple of grains between thumbnail and fingernail. If a watery liquid squirts out then the cob is unripe. If the liquid is creamy then the cob is just right for picking, but if the contents are thick and doughy you have waited too long.

When harvesting carefully twist off the ripe cob from the stem. Do this just before it is required for cooking.

VARIETIES

TRADITIONAL varieties

Open-pollinating varieties are not as reliable as the modern F_1 hybrids and so they have almost disappeared from the catalogues. Sugar-enhanced varieties remain in peak condition longer than the standard types — early-maturing varieties are the ones to grow in less than ideal conditions.

CHAMP One of the sugar-enhanced sweet corn varieties — early-maturing and reliable in colder areas.

HONEY BANTAM A bicoloured F_1 hybrid — kernels are a mixture of yellow and pale cream. Matures very early.

INCREDIBLE This sugar-enhanced F_1 hybrid bears unusually long cobs. Good flavour.

KELVEDON GLORY An old favourite with large well-filled cobs recommended for flavour.

MINOR A mini-corn for harvesting when the cobs are about 8 cm long. Boil or stir-fry. Minipop is a similar variety.

SUNDANCE This F_1 hybrid matures early and is a good choice for northern areas.

SUNRISE An F_1 hybrid with heavy cobs. Compact growth habit — useful for small plots.

SUPERSWEET varieties

The kernels contain about twice the amount of sugar as the traditional types. They have less vigour, so should not be sown until early June. Do not grow near a traditional type.

CONQUEST More vigorous and resistant to cold conditions than most other supersweet varieties.

DICKSON A sweet corn giant — 2 m high with cobs up to 20 cm long. Very early.

EARLY XTRA SWEET One of the first of the supersweets. Early and tasty, but the cobs are not well-filled.

SWEET 77 A midseason variety with very large cobs. Yields and vigour are only moderate.

Kelvedon Glory

Sweet 77

Honey Bantam

TOMATO, GREENHOUSE

No other greenhouse fruit or vegetable can match the popularity of tomatoes. Most households have a constant requirement for both raw and cooked ones, but this universal appeal for growing your own is a little surprising. It is a demanding crop, with pots and growing bags needing daily watering in summer. It is also a troublesome crop, with a wide range of pests and diseases finding the plant an ideal host. The key is obviously the fascination of watching tiny green pinheads swelling into bright red fruits. The greenhouse varieties are cordon (single-stemmed) plants which require support and reach 2 m or more if not stopped. New varieties appear every year — try an unusual one for a change.

Expected germination time	8 - 11 days
Expected yield per plant	4 kg
Approximate time between sowing and picking	16 weeks
Ease of cultivation	Not easy

CALENDAR

Heated greenhouse: Sow seed in late December and plant into permanent quarters in late February or early March for a May - June crop. Keep the house at a minimum of 10° - 12°C at night.

Cold greenhouse: Tomatoes are usually grown in an unheated ('cold') house. Sow seed in early March and plant in late April or early May. The first fruits will be ready for picking in July.

Month	JAN	FEB	MAR	APR	MAY	JUN	JUL	AUG	SEP	OCT	NOV	DEC
Sowing & Planting (Heated greenhouse)	▦	🌱🌱										▦
Sowing & Planting (Cold greenhouse)			▦▦	🌱🌱								
Picking Time												

SOWING & PLANTING THE CROP

The traditional way to grow tomatoes under glass was to plant the seedlings in the border soil in the greenhouse. Watering and feeding with this method of cultivation is more straightforward than with the more modern growing techniques, but there is a serious problem. Pests and diseases build up in the soil, which means that border soil must be either sterilised or changed every couple of seasons.

Because of this difficulty it is usual to choose an alternative method. Growing in 10 or 15 litre pots filled with potting compost is a simple technique, but growing bags have taken over as the most popular growing system.

Follow the conventional technique of sowing thinly in trays or pans filled with a suitable compost if you need a large number of plants. Cover the seeds lightly with compost — keep moist but not wet at about 18°C. When the seedlings have produced a pair of true leaves prick them out into 8 cm compost-filled peat pots. If only a few plants are required, it is easier to sow a couple of seeds in each 8 cm peat pot of compost, removing the weaker seedlings after germination.

Plant out in pots, growing bags or border soil when the seedlings are 15 - 20 cm high and the flowers of the first truss are beginning to open. Water before planting. Plant 45 cm apart in the border.

LOOKING AFTER THE CROP

Tie the main stem loosely to a cane or wind it up a well-anchored but slack vertical string. Cut off or pinch out side shoots when they are about 3 cm long.

Remove the leaves below the first truss when the plants are about 1.2 m tall. Use a sharp knife to take off yellowing leaves below the fruit trusses as the season progresses. Do not overdo this deleafing process.

Water regularly to keep the compost moist but not saturated at all times. Feed with a soluble tomato fertilizer — follow the manufacturer's instructions.

Mist the plants and tap the supports occasionally to aid pollen dispersal and fruit set. Ventilate and shade the glass in summer. Remove the tip at 2 leaves above the top truss when the plants have reached the top of the house or when 7 trusses have set.

HARVESTING THE CROP

Follow the rules set out on page 107.

VARIETIES

Cherry tomatoes are bite-sized and full of flavour. Beefsteak varieties are large and meaty — stop the plants at the fourth truss. Between these two are the majority of varieties — the standard round tomato. Finally there are the novelty types, which are either non-round or non-red. Several old favourites keep their place in the catalogues, but F$_1$ hybrids are generally higher yielding and have better disease resistance.

AILSA CRAIG Standard. Popular bright red variety, recommended for its flavour.

ALICANTE Standard. Early cropping variety. Noted for its reliability and heavy cropping. Good flavour.

BIG BOY Beefsteak. The most popular giant tomato, producing fruit weighing 500 gm or more.

GARDENER'S DELIGHT Cherry. One of the first cherry varieties — still widely grown for its tangy-sweet fruits.

GOLDEN SUNRISE Novelty. The usual choice for the gardener who wants a yellow tomato. Medium-sized fruit.

MONEYMAKER Standard. One of the old favourites. Large trusses of heavy fruit, but the flavour is bland.

NECTAR Cherry. A 'vine-ripened' tomato — fruits stay firm for 2 weeks after ripening.

SANTA Novelty. Plum-shaped mini-tomatoes — this F$_1$ variety carries up to 50 fruits on a truss.

SHIRLEY Standard. An F$_1$ hybrid which is hard to beat — early cropping, fine flavour and good disease resistance.

SUNGOLD Cherry. Orange-coloured mini-tomatoes rated by some experts as the sweetest of all.

SWEET MILLION Cherry. Up to 50 supersweet fruits per truss — try it as a change from Gardener's Delight.

TIGERELLA Novelty. An early-maturing tomato which bears red and yellow stripes when mature. Good flavour.

Ailsa Craig

Big Boy

TOMATO, OUTDOOR

If you live in a mild area and there is some shelter from cold winds then you can expect a satisfactory crop in the open garden in most summers. The outdoor crop has its benefits — the flavour of the fruit is generally better and the bush varieties take some of the hard work out of tomato growing. There are several points to watch. First of all, make sure you choose a variety which is recommended for growing outdoors. Next, you must prepare the ground properly — this crop needs well-drained, humus-rich soil. Finally, remember to remove the growing point of a cordon variety while the plant is quite small — see page 107. Leaving it to grow to its full height will prevent the fruits from ripening.

Expected germination time	8 - 11 days
Expected yield per plant	2 kg
Life expectancy of stored seed	3 years
Approximate time between sowing and picking	20 weeks
Ease of cultivation	Not easy

CALENDAR

The usual time for sowing seed under glass is in late March or early April. The young plants are hardened off during May and planted out in early June, or late May if the danger of frost has passed. Plants to be grown under cloches are set out in mid May.

Under average conditions the first tomatoes will be ready for picking in mid August.

Month	JAN	FEB	MAR	APR	MAY	JUN	JUL	AUG	SEP	OCT	NOV	DEC
Sowing & Planting Time			▣	▣	❧❧							
Picking Time								▓				

SOWING & PLANTING THE CROP

Choose a spot in front of a south-facing wall if you can. Dig thoroughly and incorporate garden compost in winter. Shortly before planting rake in a general-purpose fertilizer.

You can grow outdoor tomatoes in 15 litre pots or in compost-filled growing bags. These can be placed on the open ground or on a patio. Remember that container growing calls for regular feeding and much more frequent watering than growing in a bed or border.

If you plan to buy seedlings rather than raising your own, pick ones which are dark green, sturdy and about 20 cm tall. These young plants should be pot grown.

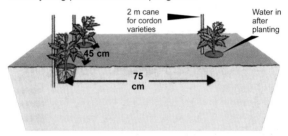

Plant out into growing bags, pots or the vegetable plot when the flowers of the first truss are beginning to open. Water the seedling before planting out and make sure that the top of the soil ball is set just below the soil surface.

You will get a better crop if you spread black plastic sheeting over the soil and plant through X-shaped slits.

LOOKING AFTER THE CROP

With a cordon variety tie the stem loosely to the cane. Make the ties at 30 cm intervals as the plant grows. Side shoots will appear where the leaf stalks join the stem. Pinch them out when they are about 3 cm long. Remove yellowing leaves below fruit trusses as the season progresses, but never overdo this deleafing process. When small tomatoes have developed on the 4th truss remove the tip at 2 leaves above this truss.

With all varieties water regularly in dry weather to keep the soil moist — alternating dryness and flooding will cause blossom end rot or fruit splitting.

HARVESTING THE CROP

Pick the fruits when they are ripe and fully coloured. Hold the tomato in your palm and with your thumb break off the fruit at the knuckle (swelling on the stalk).

At the end of the season remove the green fruits and place them in a tray. Put them in a drawer — next to the tray set a couple of ripe apples which will generate the ripening gas ethylene.

VARIETIES

CORDON varieties

These varieties are grown as single stems. As with green-house tomatoes there are cherry, standard, beefsteak and novelty types — see page 105. Some of the varieties on page 105 can be grown outdoors — these are Ailsa Craig, Alicante, Gardener's Delight, Golden Sunrise, Moneymaker, Sweet Million, Sungold and Tigerella.

MARMANDE Beefsteak. The irregular-shaped fruits are large and fleshy with few seeds.

OUTDOOR GIRL Standard. One of the first tomatoes to ripen — widely recommended as one of the best outdoor varieties.

YELLOW PERFECTION Novelty. Yellow standard-sized tomatoes — the best yellow for growing outdoors.

BUSH varieties

These varieties are either bushes 30 - 75 cm tall or creeping plants less than 25 cm high. They do not require supporting, trimming or stopping and are excellent for cloche culture. Straw or plastic sheeting must be laid around the plants as many fruits are at ground level.

INCAS Novelty. This F_1 hybrid produces plum-shaped fruits. Early ripening. Good tolerance of wilt diseases.

RED ALERT Cherry. Larger than the usual cherry tomato with a flavour that beats the other bush varieties.

ROMA Novelty. Plum-shaped fleshy fruit which are almost seedless. Good for cooking.

THE AMATEUR Standard. The 40 cm high bush bears a heavy crop of medium-sized tomatoes. Moderate flavour.

TINY TIM Cherry. A dwarf bush you can plant in a windowbox. Fruits are almost seedless.

TORNADO Cherry. Quite similar to Red Alert, but fruits appear a little later. Yields are high.

TUMBLER Cherry. The variety to grow in hanging baskets and containers — trailing stems bear masses of fruit.

Marmande

Tiny Tim

TURNIP

Turnips are not just for use in casseroles and stews. Early varieties are sown in spring and pulled when they are the size of golf balls for eating raw in salads or for boiling whole for the dinner plate. Maincrop varieties can be sown in the autumn and the tops cut for spring greens when winter is over. An easy-to-grow and quick-maturing crop, but remember that the early varieties are more demanding than the maincrop ones — any check due to poor drainage, lack of nutrients, dryness at the roots etc will drastically reduce both tenderness and flavour.

Expected germination time	6 - 10 days
Approximate number of seeds per 10 gm	3000
Expected yield from a 3 m row	3 kg (early vars.)
Expected yield from a 3 m row	5 kg (maincrop vars.)
Life expectancy of stored seed	3 years
Approximate time between sowing and lifting	6 - 12 weeks
Ease of cultivation	Easy

CALENDAR

Early varieties: Sow Purple-top Milan under cloches in February and other early turnips in open ground between March and June for a May - September crop.

Maincrop varieties: Sow between mid July and mid August for cropping and storage from mid October onwards.

Turnip tops: Sow a maincrop variety in August or September for a supply of spring greens in March and April which are more nutritious than spinach.

Month	JAN	FEB	MAR	APR	MAY	JUN	JUL	AUG	SEP	OCT	NOV	DEC
Sowing Time												
Lifting Time			TOPS ONLY									

SOWING THE CROP

Turnips belong to the cabbage family and like the other members require a firm, non-acid soil which has reasonable drainage. Early varieties require the soil to be fertile — these early ones are not suitable for sandy or shallow ground.

Pick a non-shady spot and dig in autumn — lime if necessary. In spring apply a general-purpose fertilizer and prepare the seed bed about a week later.

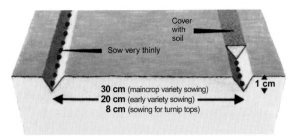

Cover with soil

Sow very thinly

30 cm (maincrop variety sowing)
20 cm (early variety sowing)
8 cm (sowing for turnip tops)

1 cm

LOOKING AFTER THE CROP

Thin out turnips which are being grown for roots as soon as the seedlings are large enough to handle. Do this in stages until the plants are 25 cm (maincrop varieties) or 15 cm (early varieties) apart. Do not thin turnips which are being grown for their tops.

Keep down the weeds by hoeing around the plants and remember to water during periods of dry weather — failure to do so will result in small and woody roots. Rain following a dry spell can cause the roots to crack if the soil has not been watered.

Spray with an insecticide at the first signs of flea beetle damage (small round holes in the leaves).

HARVESTING THE CROP

The roots of early varieties should be pulled out of the ground like radishes rather than being levered out with a fork like swedes. Pull while the roots are still small — golf-ball size if they are to be eaten raw or between golf-ball and tennis-ball size if they are to be cooked.

Begin lifting maincrop turnips as soon as they are large enough to use — remember that tenderness and flavour decrease with age. Harvesting usually begins in October and in most areas you can leave them in the ground and lift as required. In cold and wet areas it is preferable to lift in early November — twist off the leaves and place the roots between layers of sand in a stout box. Store in a cool shed.

Cut the tops of turnips grown for spring greens in March or April when about 15 cm high. Leave the plants to resprout — several cuts can be obtained.

VARIETIES

EARLY varieties

These varieties are quick-maturing and should be pulled when the roots are still young and tender. They are not suitable for storing and should be used within a few days of harvesting.

ARCOAT The red-topped white roots have a flattish top — not easy to find.

ATLANTIC A selected strain of Purple-top Milan which has a longer sowing and harvesting period.

IVORY Something different — a cylindrical white turnip. Sow in the open garden from mid March or under glass in February.

MARKET EXPRESS An F_1 hybrid of the Tokyo Cross type which quickly produces small white globes.

PURPLE-TOP MILAN A flat, white turnip with a purple top. The earliest of the popular varieties.

SNOWBALL A favourite variety — quick-growing, globular and white fleshed. Good for growing under cloches.

SPRINTER A selected strain of Purple-top Milan which is slightly smaller and claimed to be even earlier.

TOKYO CROSS Sow in May - August for small white globes ready for pulling in about 6 weeks.

MAINCROP varieties

These varieties are larger and slower to mature than the earlies — they are also hardier and can be lifted and stored for winter and spring use. There are not many varieties on offer.

CHAMPION GREEN-TOP YELLOW Yellow-fleshed like Golden Ball, but it appears in few catalogues.

GOLDEN BALL The only maincrop you are likely to find in the popular catalogues. Yellow-fleshed roots.

GREEN-TOP WHITE Large and green-topped — the variety recommended for use as spring greens.

MANCHESTER MARKET A typical white-fleshed green top. The variety recommended for prolonged storage.

Snowball

Green-top White

CHAPTER 3

BABY VEGETABLES

The terms 'baby vegetable' and 'mini-vegetable' have been coined to describe the miniature sweet corn, french beans etc packed in small trays at your local supermarket. These products are quite expensive and it is nice to know that you can grow your own. There are just a few simple rules to follow.

There are two distinct types of baby vegetable. Firstly there are standard varieties which are grown closely together and harvested at an early stage. They are generally quick-maturing types such as Amsterdam Forcing (carrot) and Snowball (turnip). Secondly there are a number of varieties which have been specifically bred as baby vegetables. They are the true miniatures — examples include Idol (cauliflower) and Protovoy (savoy cabbage). These varieties are usually described and illustrated in a separate section of the seed catalogue.

Both these types are grown more closely together than standard varieties. The usual distance between the rows is 15 cm, but you will need more space for bigger plants such as sweet corn and courgettes. The distance between the plants after thinning is 3 cm for roots (carrot, beetroot etc), 15 cm for lettuce and cabbage and 30 cm for sweet corn.

With these greatly reduced planting distances baby vegetables are extremely useful where space is limited. They make growing your own food in pots, troughs, tiny beds and window boxes a practical proposition, but there is an important point to bear in mind. Baby vegetables need to be grown quickly, so use a reliable brand of compost or humus-rich soil and feed them regularly. Water the growing medium thoroughly when the weather is dry.

Turnip — Tokyo Cross

Cabbage — Protovoy

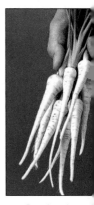
Parsnip — Lancer

Included here are varieties which have been specifically bred as baby vegetables, together with some standard varieties which can be harvested at an early stage.

VEGETABLE	VARIETY
BEETROOT	Detroit 2 - Little Ball Monaco Nero Pronto
BRUSSELS SPROUT	Energy
CABBAGE (SAVOY)	Protovoy
CAPSICUM	Minibel
CARROT	Amini Ideal Parmex Suko
CAULIFLOWER	Idol
COURGETTE	Patriot Supremo
CUCUMBER	Petita
FRENCH BEAN	Masai Safari
KALE	Showbor
KOHL RABI	Logo Rolando
LEEK	Jolant King Richard
LETTUCE	Blush Minigreen Sherwood Tom Thumb
ONION	Imai Senshyu Shakespeare
PARSNIP	Arrow Lancer
SPINACH	Teton
SQUASH	Peter Pan Sunburst
SWEET CORN	Minipop
TOMATO	Gardener's Delight Red Alert Tiny Tim Tumbler
TURNIP	Arcoat Tokyo Cross

Leek — King Richard

Carrot — Amini

Cauliflower — Idol

CHAPTER 4

GETTING STARTED

CROP ROTATION

Do not grow a vegetable in the same spot year after year. If you do then soil pests and diseases will increase and soil nutrient levels will become unbalanced. Crop rotation is the answer and the standard 3 year plan is shown below. If this seems like too much trouble follow a very simple routine — roots this year, an above-ground vegetable on that ground next year and then back to a root crop.

ROOTS
beetroot • carrot • chicory parsnip • potato

Do not add manure.

Do not lime.

Star need Rake in a general-purpose fertilizer about 2 weeks before sowing or planting.

BRASSICAS
broccoli • brussels sprout cabbage • cauliflower • kale kohl rabi • radish • swede • turnip

Add some well-rotted manure or compost at digging time if soil is known to be short of humus.

Star need Lime the soil unless you are sure it is already alkaline.

Star need Rake in a general-purpose fertilizer about 2 weeks before sowing or planting.

OTHERS
aubergine • bean • capsicum celeriac • celery • cucumber endive • leaf beet • leek • lettuce marrow • onion • pea • spinach sweet corn • tomato

Star need Add a liberal amount of well-rotted manure or compost at digging time.

Lime only if the soil is known to be acid.

Rake in a general-purpose fertilizer about 2 weeks before sowing or planting.

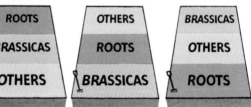

YEAR 1 YEAR 4 ...	YEAR 2	YEAR 3
ROOTS	OTHERS	BRASSICAS
BRASSICAS	ROOTS	OTHERS
OTHERS	BRASSICAS	ROOTS

MANURING

The purpose of increasing the humus content of the soil is to improve the crumb structure and to increase the water- and food-holding capacity. In autumn or early winter spread bulky organic matter over the surface — apply 5 kg per sq. m (approximately 1 barrowload per 8 sq. m). The area chosen should be for crops other than roots or brassicas, but old compost can be used to enrich all land if it is starved of humus.

Animal manure is not always easy to find and the answer is to make as much compost as you can, using both garden and kitchen waste. Make sure some carbon-rich matter (straw, leaves, chopped newspaper etc) is present, and remember to keep the heat in and the rain out. Do not use lime but add a little soil between the organic matter layers.

Fork the organic matter into the soil before digging starts if time allows. The object should be to enrich part of the vegetable plot each year until the whole area has been treated.

DIGGING

The time for digging is during a dry spell in late autumn or early winter if you plan to sow or plant in spring — don't try to dig and make a seed bed in one operation. Dig out a trench about 45 cm wide and 1 spit (spade-depth) deep at the front of the plot and move the soil to the back. Spread compost over the surface of the area to be enriched with humus. Now begin to dig the plot — invert a 10 - 15 cm wide strip of soil into the trench in front. Move backwards, turning over each successive strip until a final trench is formed. Fill this with the soil brought over from the first trench. Some keen vegetable growers double dig once every 3 years in order to break up the compacted layer below the depth of digging. This calls for forking over the bottom of each trench before turning over the soil from the adjacent strip.

DIGGING TIPS

- Choose a spade which is suited to your height and strength. Keep the blade clean.

- Choose the right day. The ground must be neither frozen nor saturated.

- Begin slowly. For most people 30 minutes on the first day is quite enough.

- Insert the blade of the spade vertically, not at an angle. Turn in annual weeds but remove roots of perennial ones.

- Leave the soil in clods — frost will break down most of them during the winter months.

- Never bring subsoil to the surface — chalk, raw clay or sand will ruin the fertility.

THE TRADITIONAL PLOT

The traditional plot remains the standard way of growing vegetables at home. The whole of the area is cultivated and the plants are grown in rows. Strips of bare earth are left between each row or group of rows so that the gardener is able to walk along for weeding, picking etc. By this method the longest broad beans, the heaviest cabbages and so on are produced, and the textbooks assume that you are going to follow this method when giving you cultural instructions.

Despite its popularity the traditional plot may not be the best method of growing vegetables for you unless you want to grow bigger ones than your neighbours or win prizes at the horticultural show. The bed system (pages 120 - 121) has several important advantages.

PREPARING THE SEED BED

The pattern for most vegetables is to sow seeds outdoors and then either leave them to grow where sown or else transplant them as seedlings to another spot where they are left to grow to maturity. Either way a seed bed is required.

Early spring is the usual time to start, but you must wait until the soil is workable. The surface will have started to change colour but it will still be moist just below this thin dry layer. Walk over the plot — if the soil sticks to your footwear then it is still too wet.

The first task is to break down the clods which you brought up with the winter digging. Use a hand cultivator or garden fork — work on a push - pull principle to break the large lumps and roughly level the surface. Do not let the prongs go deeper than 15 cm. Repeat the cultivation at right angles if the surface is still very uneven and clods are still present.

The next step is to apply a dressing of fertilizer. It is unwise to leave all of this dressing on the surface as in concentrated form it can damage the tiny roots of the germinating seeds. To avoid this risk work the fertilizer into the top few centimetres with a rake or hand cultivator.

Now you are ready to prepare the seed bed, and the rules have changed in recent years. The traditional way was to tread over the surface in order to consolidate the lower levels and then to squash any remaining clods. The final step was to rake over the surface until it was smooth.

Nowadays treading is frowned upon because it has been shown to damage the soil structure, so follow the new rules. Walk normally over the surface with a rake and use it to fill in the hollows and break down the mounds. Pick up debris and small stones. When you have finished this operation, use the rake in a push - pull fashion to produce a smooth and level seed bed with a crumbly surface. These crumbs should not be too small. A surface with the consistency of coarse breadcrumbs should be your goal — the larger the seed, the less the need for a fine crumb structure.

LIMING

The addition of organic matter and fertilizers plus heavy cropping tends to increase the acidity of the soil. Never lime every year as a matter of routine — if you are following the standard crop rotation plan then lime only the land which is to be used for brassicas. This means that the land is limed once every 3 years — see page 114.

There is no need to guess the amount of lime to use — a simple pH kit will tell you the degree of acidity and this reading plus the soil type determine the application rate. This will be 250 - 750 gm per sq. m. If you don't want to go to the trouble of testing, use 250 gm per sq. m. The experts recommend ground limestone rather than hydrated lime.

Timing is all-important. Sprinkle the lime over the freshly-dug surface if organic matter has not been added — do not incorporate into the soil. If manure has been added, postpone liming until February. Lime likes to be alone, and that means not mixing with fertilizers as well as manure. Feeding should take place either a month before or after liming.

SEED SOWING

Proper timing is extremely important — not too early, not too deeply and not too thickly are the golden rules. The calendars in this book will give you approximate times but your own soil and weather conditions must set the precise time. Seed will germinate only when the temperature is high enough to allow growth to begin — sowing in wet, near-freezing soil is bound to lead to disaster.

Mark out the row with a length of taut string. With a stick, trowel or the edge of a hoe draw out a drill to the recommended depth. Feel the soil at the bottom of the drill — water gently through the rose of a watering can if it is dry. Sow seed as thinly as you can along the row. Do not do this directly from the packet — place some seeds in the palm of your hand and gently sprinkle using your thumb and forefinger. Fine seed should be mixed with sand before sowing.

When the drill has been sown, cover the seed by carefully replacing the soil using the back of a rake. If you are not skilled at this operation it is better to push the soil back with your fingers. Firm the replaced soil but do not water. If the weather is dry then cover the surface with newspaper.

Large seeds such as sweet corn, marrow and broad beans are either sown in a drill or in holes dug with a trowel or dibber at the stations where they are to grow. It is good practice to sow 2 or 3 seeds at each station, thinning all but the strongest seedling after germination.

- Open-pollinated seed: Most varieties are of this 'standard' type. No specialist hybridisation has been involved.

- F_1 hybrid seed: A variety produced by crossing pure-bred parents. Increased vigour and uniformity of shape etc are the major features — generally more expensive.

GETTING MORE FROM THE PLOT

The instructions so far have been to follow a rotational plan and in each allotted area to grow the vegetables of your choice at the spacings recommended in the A - Z guide. You can, however, increase the overall yield from your plot by using one or more of the techniques described below.

SUCCESSIONAL SOWING

Several vegetables, such as lettuces and radishes, cannot be stored for later use. To avoid a glut and then a famine it is necessary to sow short rows of your chosen variety every few weeks. A boon for the gardener who does not want to do this are the 'mixed seed' packets offered by many suppliers. The mixture of early- and late-maturing varieties will give you a prolonged harvesting period from a single sowing.

CATCH CROPPING

Purple-sprouting broccoli will have come to the end in April or early May — early peas will be finished by late June or July. Catch cropping is the answer to summer-long bare ground. Fork over the area and level the surface with a rake. Sow a quick-maturing crop such as spring onions, radishes, dwarf lettuce, beetroots, turnips or french beans. The crop will be harvested before the time for autumn digging and the rotational plan will not be disturbed.

INTERSOWING

This useful double-purpose technique involves mixing the seed of a compact and quick-growing crop such as radish or Tom Thumb lettuce with a slow-maturing crop such as parsnips. The radish or lettuce seedlings emerge quickly and mark out the row — an important advantage when hoeing. Thin out as normal. The radish or lettuce will be ready for harvesting long before the parsnips have developed to the stage of needing the space occupied by the quick-growing marker plants.

INTERCROPPING

Intercropping is a neater method than intersowing for making maximum use of the land earmarked for a slow-growing crop. Between adjacent rows of slow developers such as brussels sprouts, leeks and parsnips sow a row of a crop which will be harvested in summer before the prime crop needs the space. Popular intercroppers are radishes, early peas, early carrots, spinach and dwarf lettuce. Make sure that the intercropping vegetable has enough room — the space between the rows must be wide enough to allow easy passage. If necessary widen the recommended row space of the prime crop if you plan to sow an intercrop.

GROWING IN CONTAINERS

There are good and bad points about growing vegetables in containers such as pots, troughs and growing bags. On the credit side there are no poor soil problems, no weeding and digging worries, and no soil pest attacks. On the drawback side the amount you can grow is strictly limited and most vegetables have no decorative value, but the major problem is the need for regular watering and feeding. Pots should be raised above the ground or paving to allow free drainage.

GROWING IN THE GREENHOUSE

The usual reason for growing vegetables in a greenhouse is the ability to grow those types which are unpredictable outdoors and even impossible in some areas — aubergine, capsicum and tomatoes are examples. In addition there is the satisfaction of harvesting produce before the outdoor crop is ready — early potatoes, early carrots and so on. There is one other advantage — the ability to sow, care for the plants and harvest the crop in a pleasant environment without having to worry about rain, wind and snow.

A large number of ornamentals need a cool (minimum temperature 7°C) or a warm (minimum temperature 12°C) greenhouse for satisfactory growth, but all the popular vegetables can be grown in an unheated greenhouse. All too often you find just a few growing bags of tomatoes — remember that there are also aubergines, winter lettuce, cucumbers, okra etc. Early in the season the space between tomatoes and cucumbers can be utilised for quick-growing catch crops such as early carrots. Remember to check that the varieties of tomatoes, cucumbers and lettuce are recommended for growing under glass.

The greenhouse has an additional role to play. It can be used to give outdoor varieties an early start in life by sowing them in a propagator, pricking out into pots and then planting outdoors to give them a start of several weeks over garden-grown specimens.

THE BED SYSTEM

Anyone who has looked after an allotment will know that the traditional plot (page 116) is hard work. Annual digging is necessary because of the tramping down of the soil along the pathways — regular weeding is necessary because of the spaces between the rows of plants. The bed system involves much less effort — the yield per plant is of course less than you would expect by the traditional long row method, but the yield per sq. metre is often higher.

The basic principle is to create a series of rectangular beds which are divided by permanent paths. These paths are covered with gravel or bark chippings and the beds must be narrow enough so that all the plants can be reached from the paths. If possible construct the beds so that they run north to south.

Organic matter is added to the soil and it should be left to settle for a couple of weeks before sowing or planting. The yearly round begins in autumn or early winter when a top-up layer of organic matter such as well-rotted manure or garden compost is worked into the surface with a fork. Digging is not necessary as you have not trodden down the soil by walking on it.

Choose your vegetables from the A - Z guide. As a general rule it is a good idea to pick dwarf and early-maturing varieties — on page 121 is a list of easy-to-grow vegetables which are ideal for the bed system. Note that the plants are grown at the same distance from each other in both directions. This space is quite small so that the leaves of adjacent plants touch when they are mature.

Looking after the crop during the growing season is usually a relatively simple job. There are no muddy walkways between the plants and the closeness of the vegetables means that most weeds are smothered.

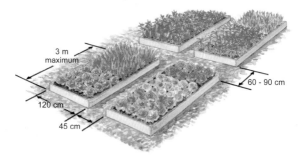

On free-draining soil you can create ground-level beds between the pathways. If drainage is poor then you need raised beds — see above. The bed should be at least 10 cm high — retaining walls of bricks, blocks, railway sleepers or pressure-treated planks are necessary. Fork over the bottom and fill with a mixture of 2 parts topsoil and 1 part organic matter. Put black plastic sheeting below the path covering of bark or gravel.

EASY VEGETABLES FOR THE BED SYSTEM

VEGETABLE	SOW or PLANT	DEPTH	DISTANCE BETWEEN PLANTS	HARVEST
BEAN, BROAD	February - April	5 cm	15 cm	July - August
Begin picking when pods are 8 cm long — cook whole				
BEAN, FRENCH	May - June	5 cm	15 cm	July - September
Pencil-podded varieties are popular				
BEETROOT	April - June	3 cm	8 cm	June - October
Grow a globe variety				
CALABRESE	April - May	1 cm	38 cm	August - September
Express Corona is a good choice				
CARROT	March - July	1 cm	10 cm	July - October
Pick a quick-maturing short-rooted variety				
COURGETTE	May - June	3 cm	45 cm	July - September
Cut when 8 - 10 cm long				
LETTUCE	March - July	1 cm	24 cm	June - October
Grow a miniature or loose-leaf variety				
ONION	March - April	Tip showing	8 cm	August
Grow sets rather than seed				
POTATO	March - April	10 cm	30 cm	June - July
Grow an early variety for new potatoes				
RADISH	March - July	1 cm	5 cm	May - September
Nothing is easier to grow				
TOMATO	June	—	45 cm	August - September
Choose a bush variety				
TURNIP	March - June	1 cm	15 cm	May - September
Grow an early variety — pick at golf-ball size				

DISTANCE BETWEEN PLANTS

These spacings are the recommended distance between rows and also between mature plants in the rows.

CHAPTER 5

PLANT CARE

THINNING

Despite the recommendation to sow thinly you will usually find that the emerged seedlings are too close together. Thinning is necessary, and this task should be tackled as soon as the plants are large enough to handle. The soil should be moist — gently water if necessary. Hold down the soil around the unwanted seedling with one hand and pull it up with the other. If the seedlings are too close together to allow this technique, nip off the top growth of the unwanted plants.

After thinning, firm the soil around the remaining seedlings and water gently. This thinning is often done in stages until the final spacing is reached.

TRANSPLANTING

Transplanting involves moving seedlings to their permanent home where they will grow to maturity. These transplants may have been raised in a seed bed in the garden, bought from a garden centre or grown indoors in pots or trays. It is a temptation to use thinnings and plant them elsewhere, but transplanting is not suitable for all vegetables. It is firmly recommended for most members of the cabbage family, acceptable for some popular crops such as peas and beans but definitely not recommended for many others such as lettuce and root crops.

Water both the seedlings and the site where they are to be grown on the day before transplanting. Set the plants at the depth they were in the seed bed or pot. Firm the soil around the plants and water in to settle the roots. Water again if there is a dry spell after planting.

Transplanting is a vital time in the plant's life and choosing the right time is important. Cold, wet soil can be fatal and so can late frosts for half-hardy vegetables.

MULCHING

Mulching is an in-season method of manuring. A 3 - 5 cm layer of well-rotted manure or leaf mould is spread between the young plants once they are established in spring. The mulch reduces water loss, increases nutrient content, improves soil structure and helps to suppress weeds. Before application cultivate and water the surface so that it will be moist, weed-free and friable.

WATERING

Dryness of the soil around the roots is one of the most serious problems the vegetable grower may have to face. The lack of water during a prolonged dry spell can result in a small crop or even no crop at all. In addition heavy rain following this period of drought results in the splitting of tomatoes and roots.

The answer is to ensure that the soil around the roots is not allowed to become dry. The first step is to incorporate adequate organic matter into the soil — this increases the water-holding capacity. Next, make sure that the top 20 cm of soil is thoroughly moist but not waterlogged at sowing or planting time. Finally, put down a mulch (see page 122) in late spring.

You now have done all you can to ensure a good moisture reserve in your soil — the rest is up to the weather. If there is a prolonged dry spell then watering will be necessary, especially for tomatoes, marrows, beans, peas, celery and onions.

The rule is to water the soil gently and thoroughly every 7 days when the weather is dry during the critical period. This is the time between flowering and full pod development for peas and beans, and from seedling to maturity for leaf crops. Apply 10 litres per sq. m when **overall watering**. Water slowly and close to the base of the plants — try to water in the morning rather than at midday or in the evening. A watering can is often used, but you need a hosepipe if watering is not to be a prolonged chore. One of the most effective ways of watering is to use lay-flat perforated tubing or a leaky-pipe watering system between the rows.

Where there is only a limited number of plants you would do better to use **point watering**. This involves inserting an empty plant pot or making a depression in the soil around each stem. Water is then poured into the pot or depression.

The main reason for disappointment with growing bags is due to trying to follow the traditional technique used for watering the vegetable plot. Keeping the compost properly moist in a growing bag is a different technique, and you should follow the maker's instructions carefully.

FEEDING

A number of chemical elements are essential for plant growth. Three are required in relatively large amounts — nitrogen for leaf growth, phosphorus for root development and potash for strengthening resistance to disease and poor growing conditions. A compound fertilizer contains all three of these major elements — a general-purpose fertilizer has these elements in roughly equal amounts. You will find a statement of the nutrient content on the package.

There are a number of other elements which are required in very small amounts — the trace elements. Shortage of molybdenum, boron etc can cause problems in specific vegetables, but trace element deficiency disorders are rare.

High-yield vegetables, however, are a drain on the soil's reserves of nitrogen, phosphorus and potash which means that feeding is generally necessary. Manure or fertilizer — the age-old argument. Actually there is nothing to argue about — both are vital and neither can be properly replaced by the other. The role of bulky organic matter (animal manure, garden compost etc) is to make the soil structure good enough to support a vigorous and healthy crop. The role of fertilizers is to provide the plants with enough nutrients to ensure that they reach their full potential in this soil.

One of the most important uses for compound fertilizers is to provide a **base dressing** just before sowing or planting. Use a general-purpose product such as Growmore. Crops which take some time to mature will need one or more **top dressings** during the season. Powder and granular formulations are available, but you must take care to keep such products away from leaves. It is usually better to use a liquid or soluble fertilizer — the dilute solution is applied around the plants through a watering can or hose-end dilutor.

As a time-saving alternative you can use a slow-release fertilizer — the granules, blocks or cones steadily release nutrients into the soil or compost for about 6 months.

WEEDING

Weeds give the plot an untidy appearance, but the real problem is that they compete for space, food, light and water — in addition weeds can harbour pests and diseases.

There is no single miracle cure — there are a number of tasks you will have to carry out. The first one begins before the crop is sown — at digging time remove all the roots of perennial weeds you can find and bury small annual weeds by completely inverting each spadeful of soil. If the plot has been neglected and there is a blanket of weeds you should spray with glyphosate before you begin to prepare the soil.

Additional weeds will appear among the growing plants however thoroughly you have removed the weeds before sowing or planting. Hoeing is the basic technique for keeping the problem under control — it must be carried out at regular intervals in order to keep annual weeds in constant check and to starve out the underground parts of the perennial ones. Weeds should be severed just below ground level rather than being dragged to the surface — keep the blade sharp at all times. Hoe with care — the roots of some plants lie close to the surface, and much damage can be done by hoeing deeper than 3 cm.

Chemicals have a part to play, but they must be used with care. Water on diquat/paraquat to burn off weeds between plants — paint leaves of perennial weeds with glyphosate.

SPRAYING

People who claim that they never need to spray are lying, lucky or living on poor vegetables. Pests and diseases attack well-grown as well as sickly plants — strength and vigour do not provide immunity. So buy an up-to-date guide such as The Pocket Garden Troubles Expert — this will show you what has gone wrong (not all troubles are due to pests and diseases) and it will tell you what can be done to prevent or cure the problem.

PROTECTED CROPPING

In the old days professional gardeners placed glass bell jars over plants on hot beds in order to provide out-of-season vegetables. The modern version is a clear plastic container with its bottom cut off — a simple home-made cloche.

A glass or plastic cloche will protect plants from the wind and rain while it raises the temperature of the air and soil. Sowing or planting of many vegetables can take place weeks earlier than on open ground and that means harvesting when shop prices may still be high. Half-hardy crops such as aubergine and capsicum can be grown in unfavourable areas and leafy vegetables are protected from rain and frosts in winter. Despite these virtues only 1 in 5 gardeners owns a cloche.

You will find an assortment of cloches at your local garden centre. A few rules to help you make the right choice. Match the height to the expected size of the plants as the leaves should not touch the sides — buy tent cloches for small plants and barn cloches for larger ones. Choose plastic for lightness, safety and economy — choose glass for clarity, permanence, maximum heat retention and resistance to blowing over. The corrugated PVC cloche is a good all-purpose unit, but if you want to cover large areas cheaply the answer is the plastic tunnel cloche. This is made from wire hoops and polyethylene sheeting. There is a drawback — plastic sheeting deteriorates after a few years.

Some ventilation must be provided with all cloches — increase the amount as the temperature rises. Provide ventilation by leaving gaps between the cloches, not by leaving the ends open. There is no need to remove the cloches before watering — the water will run down the sides and into the soil. Make sure that the cloches are firmly anchored into the soil and wash the glass or plastic when the surface becomes grimy. Remove the cloches when the weather is mild enough — increase ventilation for a few days in order to harden off the plants before removing their protection.

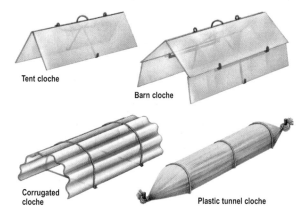

Tent cloche

Barn cloche

Corrugated cloche

Plastic tunnel cloche

HARVESTING

Many gardeners aim to produce giant vegetables to match the ones they see on the show bench, and you may therefore be surprised at some of the harvesting sizes recommended in this book. Turnips the size of a golf ball and carrots no longer than your finger — not economical for the farmer but these are the sizes for top flavour and tenderness. Not all vegetables need to be picked at an early stage — the flavour of swedes, parsnips and celery does not decline with age.

With some crops such as marrows, cucumbers, peas and beans it is essential to pick regularly as just a few ripe fruits or pods left on the plant can bring cropping to an end.

Before you begin to harvest a vegetable read what to do on the appropriate page. Carelessly tearing off pods can damage the stems of pea plants — pulling out roots by their foliage can leave part of the crop in the ground.

STORING

Nearly all vegetables can be kept for a few days or even a week or two in the refrigerator, but there will be times when long-term storage will be necessary. With beans there is always a sudden glut, and it is far better to pick them at the tender stage for storage rather than trying to extend the harvest period to the time when they will be tough and stringy.

In the pre-deep freeze era storage methods had to be devised so that a winter supply of vegetables could be provided. Peas and beans were dried and then shelled. Onions and cabbages were hung up in bags or laid out on open trays. Runner beans were salted, onions and beetroots were pickled in vinegar.

Nowadays long-term storage has been transformed by the advent of the home freezer. This is the ideal storage method for so many vegetables, including the leafy ones which cannot be kept satisfactorily by any other technique.

The routine is to blanch, cool, drain and then freeze. Blanching involves immersion in boiling water — 100 gm to 1 litre of water. Bring quickly back to the boil and continue for the recommended time (2 - 5 minutes). After blanching immerse into ice-cold water, drain thoroughly and freeze. Use freezer-grade plastic bags or other containers — exclude as much air as possible before sealing.

Maincrop roots are generally lifted in autumn for storage indoors as layers between sand or peat (e.g carrots, beetroots) or in sacks (potatoes) in a frost-free shed. You can let the vegetable plot act as a vegetable store for some roots — swedes, parsnips and turnips can be lifted as required.

The Experts —
the world's best-selling gardening books

The Bedding Plant Expert
The Bulb Expert
The Container Expert
The Easy-care Gardening Expert
The Evergreen Expert
The Flower Arranging Expert
The Flower Expert
The Flowering Shrub Expert
The Fruit Expert
The Garden Expert
The Garden DIY Expert
The Greenhouse Expert
The House Plant Expert
The Lawn Expert
The Rock & Water Garden Expert
The Rose Expert
The Tree & Shrub Expert
The Vegetable & Herb Expert